MOONLIGHT MUSIC AND YOU

WIGAN CASINO PUSHING THROUGH THE DOORS

LESTER GALLAGHER

CONTENTS

Acknowledgements

To my wife Diane, if I said I was building an Ark she would buy me the nails. She would hold those nails in place while I hit my thumb. She would laugh then tell me to try again. Richard Searling who had the good grace twenty years ago to write back to me about my first efforts of writing this book, thank you. The Wigan Observer and its journalists who reported on the Casino. The staff of Wigan library and the help I received when researching historical information. Dave Evison, Brian Rae, Keith Minshull, Soul Sam, Pat Brady, Russ Winstanley, Steve Whittle, Ginger Taylor. Their dedication and commitment to bringing the music to all those who would listen. The staff of the Casino who worked tirelessly through the night to keep us safe, fed and watered. The artists who put the music in the grooves and often never knew they had created a real classic. My sister whose Motown records were the first records I ever played and scratched without her permission. My apologies to my three children, Paul, Adam and Alisha, who had no choice but to listen to my music when traveling in the car. Little Anthony and the Imperials, who started my journey into northern soul. The DJ's and organisers that continue to work at keeping the scene alive today. Last but not least, you the reader. Dare I break with tradition and say that telling each other to 'keep the faith,' is not a slogan that fits the scene anymore? 'Faith,' is described as having conviction in something rather than proof. It has been 48 years since the writer Dave Godin christened the scene with the name 'Northern Soul,' and ended many of his columns with the phrase 'keep the faith.' The scene is now bigger and stronger than at any time in its history. The author would also like to thank the following people and agencies for their kind permission for the use of photographic material and press releases used throughout this book.

The National Library of Australia and Olav Bjaaland for the picture, Tasmanian views, Edward Searle's album of photographs of Australia, Antarctica and the Pacific, 1911-1915.

Brian Elsey for the photo taken by and entitled 'Empress Ballroom - Ron Hunt - Item # 1072 from the pages of Wigan World.

Judith Schnell of Rowman for the kind permission to use the illustration and front cover of the book Soul Survivors.

To the Editor, Janet Wilson of the Wigan Observer and all those journalists who contributed to its long and continued success. My gratitude for allowing me to include the articles taken from various dates from which the Observer reported on events associated with Wigan Casino.

The photographs used for the front and back cover of this book were taken and produced by the author of Moonlight Music and You. They may be copied or used for any other publication with prior permission from the author.

◆ ◆ ◆

Forward

My taste in music varies so much that I can go from reggae to rock in a heartbeat. Having such an open-minded approach to anything from Opera to Oasis is how I discovered Northern Soul and learnt to understand its peculiar complexities while at the same time appreciating its diversity. It's gritty and soulful but floaty and orchestral. It combines brow beaten, sorrowful desperation with uplifting, finger clicking harmonies. Seen as a passing fad in the seventies it defied the music industry and lived far beyond its expectations. Often mocked and sometimes the victim of its own success, Northern Soul and its followers were somewhat vilified. Today it has become much more widely accepted. CD's now sit on the shelves of well-known supermarkets and there are thousands of tracks and albums hosted by all the major online music providers. It's still attracting new and younger generations who have chosen to break away from the mainstream and heavily marketed club sounds. Many people who were in their youth during the seventies, and were heavily influenced by the mass marketing of commercial pop music, are now flocking to Northern Soul venues up and down the country. If you were lucky enough to have discovered this amazing music many decades ago and were one of those who stood outside the Casino with intrepid excitement on a cold Saturday night, then this book should jog a few memories. If your new to the scene, I can only say that I'm slightly jealous of the experience and the pleasure that awaits you. The secret of Northern Soul is surprisingly simple. You will hear the same records over and over again and you shall never tire of its calling. It will worm itself into your mind and wrap itself tightly around your heart, in the same way that ivy clings effortlessly to a wall. It will restore your lost energy and tap into your emotions, at the very least it will make you tap your feet. Gene Chandler had a record played at the Casino called, 'There Was a Time,' with the next line being 'I Used to Dance.'

That time belonged to a place called Wigan Casino. Behind its heavy black doors, the greatest all-night Soul venue that ever graced the UK, took place every Saturday night, for over eight years.

They danced, we danced, I danced.

Dedicated to the last remaining souls of Wigan Casino

Soul, The spiritual principle in man;

The moral and emotional part of man's nature;

Elevation of mind; fervour; essence; an inspirer;

A person.

CHAPTER 1

Follow the Cobblestone Road

For every passing decade, there are trademarks and copyrights left behind to individualise and remind you of its finest hours. As if carved in stone and left for future generations to re-discover, so historians would never be short of evidence. Rock and roll, punk rock, glam rock, folk and jazz, there is no shortage of genres and the profound figures that created and shaped their history. It is relatively easy to name the decade to the contributors. Elvis, the fifties, The Beatles the sixties, T Rex the seventies and so it shall continue. Along with the artists there were also the promoters of the scene and the current fashions, who were often as equally famous. The Colonel for Elvis, Brian Epstein, Russ Winstanley and Malcolm McLaren, monumental entrepreneurs of the music industry. At this point try to imagine the needle slipping ruthlessly across a pristine original rare 'we will rock you,' by Queen. Why is Russ Winstanley being mentioned in the same company as Brian Epstein? Are we talking about the guy who opened the doors of Wigan Casino to a world of forgotten music branded as Northern Soul? Hang on a minute, Brian Epstein gave us what many would consider the greatest band of musicians that ever lived? Imagine a court case where the barrister representing Brian Epstein would close his argument with something similar to Atticus Finch, in the novel 'to kill a mockingbird,' 'My learned friends with two hundred million albums sold worldwide and a catalogue of more number one singles than any other artist they are without doubt the greatest musicians ever recorded. Their music has been sent into the vastness of space to represent human kind. Even more astounding is the fact that they leave behind a legacy that has spanned their own original decade right through to our present day. What more evidence does a jury need? A woman takes out a fan and cools the air around her inquisitive brow. A man examines his finger nails as if to show that any further argument would be fruitless and almost a contempt of court. But there are still some members of the jury who want to hear the defence prove that Northern Soul and namely Russ Winstanley also deserve legendary status. Imagine at this point in the proceedings a judge clutching at the lapels of his red robes staring over the glasses resting at the end of his nose looking at the defence. An honest man who wants to set the record straight and ensure nothing more than a fair trial. He looks at me and with a stern voice says, 'can you please sum up for the jury, why this so called Northern Soul, should be granted legendary status?' The jury turn their heads in unison towards me like the crowd at a Wimbledon tennis match and stare hard waiting for some authentication. I've seen the movie, I walk casually towards the jury and lean on the wooden frame that surrounds them. I begin. 'What is this music that keeps on burning so bright for so long? How does something associated with a twisted wheel continue to roll on continually across the paths of generations? Why does a casino with no winners, jackpots and riches hold so much resonance with its patrons, long after its demise? The evidence is plentiful and well recorded. There are photographs, books and personal accounts that create a stirring account of all that is great about Northern Soul. With all due respect please put aside the writings of the more well-known personalities and founders of Northern Soul. Dave Godin, Stuart Cosgrove, Kev Roberts, Russ Winstanley and David Nowell. These people have been the writers with knowledgeable connections, allowing us the view from the more professional perspective. There have been films from Elaine Constantine and Shimmy Marcus

(Northern Soul 2014 & Soul Boy 2010) trying desperately to capture and recreate a slice of history that defies lights camera and action. I say defies, as it has proven to be harder to recreate the original atmosphere than the accuracy of a book. Like the scenes of a war film, the fear, death and destruction are visibly distinct, but similar to a funny story with no reaction the orator will inevitably say 'you had to be there.' I was so lucky to be there, and I want to take you back there. But not through the eyes and recollections of the many great stalwarts of the scene, but rather through the eyes and ears of the beholder. The beholder being someone who was captivated by the illusive and exclusive nature that surrounded the northern soul scene. I took part in a moment in time and had little interest in the politics and the personalities of the Casino. Like so many others I had an entirely different reason for parting with my hard-earned cash on a Saturday night. We were the foot soldiers of the scene. We were also the life blood that held it together and the very embodiment of why it still continues to breathe today. The brains were those who were smart enough to leave with money in their pockets and the brawn only left with sore feet. The brains were the people who brought us the music and went home with some cash. Deservedly so, as these were the people that searched endlessly through boxes of old records to bring us our rare vinyl that kept the scene alive. The grey matter is what separates us as humans. We think alike but possess something that also creates our individuality. But when a certain like-minded group of people get together they become a collective. When the northern soul collective came together at the right time and the right place, you suddenly had something that was explosive. It was spine tingling and exciting. It was out of this world. It was as far from the norm as one dared to be at the time. It was a mutual love of a rare kind of music along with an energetic style of dancing. In a very modern world as far removed from the Casino as you could imagine, this music still holds its own and refuses to disappear quietly away in to obscurity. So, what did I see and witness as a regular at the casino? Rest assured I'm not going to talk about engraved reference numbers etched in vinyl or which DJ pissed off another DJ. Nor will I delve into the repeated history of the Mecca versus the Casino, it meant nothing to me. The Carstairs 'It Really Hurts Me Girl, was the only thing that I associated with the Mecca.' I was told when I heard it at Wigan for the first time that this was a Mecca sound. Great tune, can I buy it? And that's where my interest ended. The so called legendary Ian Levine reminded me of the astrologist Russel Grant and therefore I couldn't care less who he was. He was renowned for going through record crates in America and finding great floor spinners to add to the scene. At the time, it never crossed my mind that these DJ's were going to the states to get these records. It seems by all accounts that certain DJ's like Ian Levine were to be found up a back alley hunting tirelessly through old record shops. For me, it always conjured up the closing scene of the 'Raiders of The Lost Ark,' with thousands of wooden crates in a giant warehouse. Something I did find interesting, although one could accuse me of being a little macabre is the stories that lie behind the artists and their demise. I found myself startlingly surprised at the cruel hand of fate that occasionally befell these great singers. The music that lends itself to northern soul is littered with despair regarding the personal tragedies that met with some of these artists. Marvin Gaye and Jackie Wilson famously met with untimely deaths, arguments and bullets. Jackie being shot by a jealous lover and amazingly survived. Tony Clarke (Landslide) being shot dead by his wife. Stuart Cosgrove's excellent book 'Northern Soul Rebels' touched on some of the fatalities that met with our great musical providers and I found it strangely fascinating. I also wondered who sang and created some of these iconic songs and where did they disappear to? Some northern soul aficionados will tell you with some derision that R Dean Taylor (Ghost in my house) was a white guy and they feel almost cheated. 'Soul singers are supposed to be black,' I've heard this unqualified announcement many times. The majority are black, (spoiler alert - Al Jolson was white and Jewish but blacked up for effect) however It must be remembered Dusty Springfield, Kiki Dee, Bobby Goldsboro and groups like Spiral Staircase (More Today Than Yesterday) are white singers and were big on the northern soul scene too. There are plenty of artists that fit this description and this is what makes northern soul so unique and sometimes difficult to fathom. Providing that you are willing to look beyond the fact that I am not a DJ, or a founder of the scene, or indeed a well-known Northern Soul celebrity, but just a journeyman qualified by membership only, then this is a good start. If you, like me, didn't see Northern Soul as some complicated underground society, but more of a great place to hang out with great music, then we have a lot in common. The fifties gave the world Rock and Roll, it helped to unite the rebellious teenager and changed the face of popular music forever. Bill Hayley rocked around the clock to what was described as the devil's music by many parents and politicians of the time. As every class of parent across the political spectrum watched their teenage children succumb to this wild and rebellious movement, there was those who also embraced this new-found freedom. The teddy boy was born and so was a new gang mentality. The desire to belong to an era that defied their parents and to leave behind the confines of social decorum and normality was growing. Romantic ballads and smooth serenades where for the older generations and the new post war period was now fostering a new-found freedom. Bing Crosby and Perry Como had crooned their way through the forties along with the Andrew Sisters and Glen Miller, who had helped keep the war effort entertained. Glen Miller disappeared on his way to France from the UK, December 15[th,] 1944, in an aeroplane that was never found. With twenty-three number one hits under his belt he left the music world with a better record than the eighteen number ones from Elvis Presley a decade later.

The fifties ripped apart the rules of conformity and raced headlong into creating what was the foundations and ground rules for all would be pop stars for decades to come. Of course, not all rock and roll stars where clad in tight pants and leather jackets with a silky quiff, but the blueprints were set in motion. Sound cool and look cool were the first rules of pop stardom, these were the image rights that were falling steadily into place. James Dean had helped solidify this image in the fifties as the movie star who had died aged just twenty-four in a car crash. This outstanding decade of music which has been richly rewarded throughout history with films and books was the precurser to what was probably considered the best music decade in history. There needs to be a special mention at this point to Little Richard who has been recognised by institutions and musical halls of fame across America and came to prominence in this decade. 'You're My Girl,' is an iconic Northern Soul sound and in my opinion, shows the great adaptability of the man.

With the oncoming advances of technology, the sixties started to take music into a journey that was indeed a magical mystery tour. This decade introduced so many variations of music that it was now impossible for the teenager not to split into new and different factions. Fashion began to play a massive part in the youth culture of the day. Expressionism became the mark of the teenager. Those who had reached their early twenties suddenly found themselves with more money in their pockets than ever before. The Mersey beat arrived and with it came The Beatles. Enough has been documented about The Beatles and their absolute dominance of the music industry. It was their experimental phases with music that enabled and prompted other musicians to diversify and look beyond the limits of a four-piece band. Across the Atlantic the birth of Motown was taking place and with it, a whole host of great singers who were set to captivate the world over. More and more phenomenal artists and groups were being produced from every corner of America and specifically Detroit, which was now on everybody's lips. The Motown sound was exceptional and Berry

Gordy had gone from car plant worker to entrepreneur overnight. His formula for success was copied all over the states and it would be true to say that we partly owe him for a large part of the catalogue of northern soul that now exists. The sound of young America was easily identifiable with its four four downbeat and snare drums. The artists were smartly dressed and vocally superior to those around them. But from around every corner there came a new group hoping to lay down a track that could change their lives forever, many of them however were doomed to failure. The artists that were spawned from this era somehow found the formula to create music and records that would not only define their own moment in time but to actually survive into future decades to come. The word legend is becoming more and more common when describing musicians, film stars and sports people. But legends never need to be identified and there are no other words to define or describe these people. Stevie Wonder, Bob Dylan, The Rolling Stones loved and admired by other artists and fans alike. How on earth do we categorise these people. Legends are supposed to be a one off, but amazingly there seems an abundance of them. The list is truly endless and today we have more and more modern performers leaving their mark for future generations. Coldplay, U2 and many others have taken music along new avenues, using modern technology to create innovative sounds with each new release. Those artists in the sixties that were rejected are not in any way to dissimilar to today's X Factor contestants who disappear quickly into the void of never having existed beyond the audition. Historically, singers and groups who managed to get as far as cutting a demo-record that flopped and disappeared into a radio station waste paper bin left behind an unusual legacy. A legacy that has outlived many of their contemporaries. A vinyl asset that lives securely in the treasured vaults of northern soul. The seventies were guilty of many misdemeanours and if there are two things that stand out it has got to be glam rock and its fashion. The seventies gave us some great music it was about fun and being extrovert. Disco was king but it sat alongside the best or worst of British, depending on your viewpoint. Mud, the Bay City Rollers, Gary Glitter, yes, we can still utter his name along with the guy who introduced him Jimmy Saville. The Sweet, Slade and Alvin Stardust, whose best achievement was teaching kids to cross the road safely and 'My Coo ca Choo. Judging from the line up mentioned previously he was probably the best man qualified for the job by all accounts. We shouldn't pour scorn on the long haired, platform shoes and make up wearing British pop star and I am talking about the men. Across the pond they were sending us their equivalent. God bless America, not only are they our favourite country cousins with our shared love of music but they sure know how to create the same shite as we do. David Cassidy, David Soul, The Osmond's, Suzi Quatro to name but a few. As influential as these performers were at the time, a small army marched to a different tune. A clandestine brotherhood looked beyond the commercialism of Top of The Pops. They had found music with a deeper meaning from Marvin Gaye such as 'What's Going On,' and other great tracks such as the Superfly album from Curtis Mayfield. There was still an abundance of talent out there producing innovative sounds, but for some reason a teenage identity crisis had surfaced and it was being swallowed up and lost in the rhetoric of media sanitisation. By this I mean the sixteen to seventeen year olds were being hit from every advertising angle possible. The marketing people of our time began to put sex into fashion with clever celebrity endorsements. Kevin Keegan was splashing the Brut all over, which became the chosen aftershave and deodorant of the Casino. It was either going to be that or old spice with Hi Karate deemed as a bit flamboyant. This is what we were being spoon-fed by the ad men, although it was a small amount of choice compared to today's markets it was beginning to have the desired impact. We had now entered the new age; 1977 Apple computers and Commodore computers were set up in January of this year and Jimmy Carter had taken over the presidency from Gerald Ford. Elvis Presley had left the planet aged forty-two, and this was the year that Saturday night fever came to the cinema. As John Travolta pointed to the ceiling and pointed to the floor, (something my two-year-old Granddaughter gets asked to do in her musical mover's class) so too did the rest of the die-hard Travolta wannabes. I gave the punks far more credit during this time of cinematic hype, as they managed to stay together as a respectable group of individuals. While Saturday night fever was breaking out across the night clubs of the UK and beer filled executives where swinging their white jackets around their heads to staying alive, we of the northern soul fraternity where getting hot under the collar with some Sunday morning amphetamine. There will be no getting away from the subject of drugs and how it became so prevalent on the northern soul scene especially at the Casino. In truth, it' doesn't warrant the publicity it was given, certainly not by today's standards. The journey that took us to the Casino was fraught with danger and it was as much a part of the excitement and history as the night itself. Like vampires we travelled in the darkness keeping hidden from the crowds. We were Intrepid travellers always wary of possible attack from any drunken corner. Like the night owls that we so often associate with our scene, we would turn our heads purposefully and wisely, glancing behind us for any would be danger. Many a journey was made alone from places such as Wigan's Wallgate train station to Station road, with some finding themselves caught up in the aggressive frenzy of the drunks in waiting. Our dress code pointed us out to the mob like a demonstrator with a white sign on a stick saying, 'come and get me,' and they did. Fists and boots flaying in the dim street lights of last orders. The risk seemed worth it to a young and agile mind and it wasn't often you travelled alone. What's more we were not afraid to fight back. I admit that I started late, four years late in fact, but I joined the Casino at the beginning of a wonderful period. I witnessed the full house, the sweat laden drug fuelled atmosphere, right down to its sad empty floors in nineteen eighty-one. I observed how the fashion changes brought us a little more dignity and heard the music go from majestic to ridiculous. I believe I know what it was truly like to breath the damp stale air of the Casino and I will shed some light on the unusual and the bizarre. Like the early morning light that shone through the top bar window at the height of the summer months beaming down like a Hollywood spotlight onto the back of the dance floor. Tiny intricacies like these stitched the fabric of the Casino together. Someone reading that last sentence who served their time at Wigan, will probably be saying, 'my god so it did.' I am no expert and I don't claim to be anything more than a bit part player in a cast of thousands, who just happened to have had a simple part beneath that spotlight that lasted four years.

◆ ◆ ◆

CHAPTER 2

Must have been a broken heart attack

Just before Russ Winstanley and David Nowell released their excellent recollections of Wigan Casino 1998, I had been piecing together what I had hoped to be the first through the key hole expose of the Casino. I had spent some long hours working through reels of microfiche scanning page by page of the Wigan Observer. As the hours at Wigan library turned into days and months I suddenly became aware that the book 'Soul Survivors, had been launched to an eager audience and I felt a tinge of despair. I felt like the explorer Robert Scot being beaten to the South Pole by Roald Amundsen, cold, late, pissed off and a wasted journey. Like all great adventurers Winstanley and Nowell had set off early and destroyed the best idea I'd had in years. Frozen and with no direction I now resembled another arctic hero, Captain Oates. He is reported to have famously said 'I'm just going outside and I may be some time,' never to have been seen again. Unlike Oates, I decided to thaw out my original writings and trudge once more into the uncharted world of writing. I stood beneath the man who wrote the book 'Soul Survivors.' I danced away my youth captivated by the sounds that really did move my soul and my feet in unison. My mother told me I'd grow out of it. I've stopped growing but like a pair of baggy hand me downs my passion for northern soul fits closer and tighter with age. A glance at the bathroom mirror confirms my age with a total lack of respect for the spirit inside. The grey hair and the grey matter work closely together to remind me that my flexibility is now limited to jogging not running. Like a mugger hiding in the shadows rheumatism waits patiently, ready to pounce and demand payback for the back drops, spins and those athletic dance floor moves that graced the sprung maple floors of the all-nighter. Deafness will affect many who remember the vibration of the bass that accompanied the sound of Eddie Spencer's 'If this is love I'd rather be lonely.' It too will drag you towards your later years with your TV turned up to the level known as 'deaf old fart.' You will become accustomed to your family saying, 'Jesus dad that's loud.' I work for a hearing aid provider, I should know. When 'I've got the need,' and 'here I go again,' are discussed with friends regarding your bladder and not a mention of Spooky Sue or Archie Bell and the Drells, then old age is cruelly confirmed. Age is nobody's friend. Age does allow us to do what older people do best and that's reminisce and exaggerate slightly. Wigan Casino was part of my life, come hell or high water I had to get there. My once lean proportioned body held no fear of the flu, I could sweat that away during eight hours of vigorous stomping. I shared the love of the music like I shared the flu virus with up to a thousand-other people. When it finally closed its doors for the last time, it left me with a void that remained difficult to fill for many years after. There was no other place like it and there never will be again.

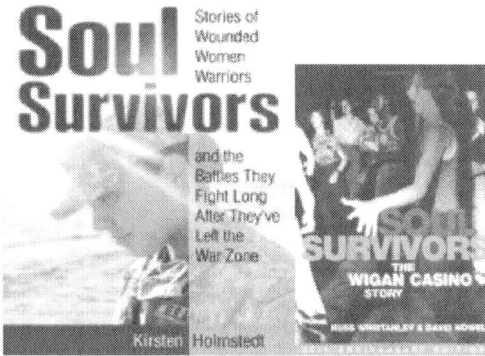

Russ Winstanley and David Nowells 'Soul Survivors' – Not to be mistaken for another 'Soul Survivors.' Which tells the stories of people and soldiers after they left the battle field. Not a single mention of the night I was attacked in the streets of Wigan on my way to the Casino.

◆ ◆ ◆

CHAPTER 3

That Driving Beat

Northern Soul was a phrase coined by the writer Dave Godin who as a journalist for the Black Echo had christened this genre of music that had no recognisable label. It stuck fast and it will be forever credited as his literary concept. It is not my intention to cover the well documented history of northern soul but rather breeze across its boughs. Its origins stretch far and wide. From its roots to its shoots, the famous clubs that paved its growth are not without their own fair share of fame and recognition. The Twisted Wheel (1963 to 1971) and The Torch (first all-nighter 1972) grew from the deep underground, like secular trees in a forest of conformity. They didn't simply sway with the wind but leaned against it defiantly. And when they were cut down in their prime they simply waited for their seeds to take root elsewhere. Councils and bye laws waited silently for the opportunity to wield the axe. It was once said from acorns grow mighty oaks and how true that was in the case of the Casino. To interpret the components of northern soul is strangely difficult. It didn't disappear with its forty-inch Spencer's and it didn't shuffle away with its customary brogues. It simply moved to a new house. Which incidentally was the title given to the new breed of music introduced in the early eighties. House music worked on the synthesised bass lines that grew out of Chicago clubs and arrived much later in the UK. Pump Up the Volume (MARRS) 1987 ignited the scene and it became the main choice of music across the clubs and bars well in to the nineties.

Wikipedia actually credits House music as *following on from the success of Northern Soul*. Great compliment if you ask me, but still begs the question, where had northern soul gone to? The answer is like doing long division, it takes some time to break it down and can be painful but eventually there's a result. Take one large number (the members of the Casino) and divide it. Wigan closed its doors and its members disbanded and they too divided. Some stayed faithfully in touch with the music by attending the small flurry of new venues that sprung up around the country including Wigan Tiffany's. Others looked upon it as the death knell of Northern Soul and when the building suspiciously caught fire it became nothing more than a funeral pyre. There was one thing that was greatly overlooked, certainly unnoticeable at the time. In fact, it was time that was needed. Living legends are extremely rare. Wealthy artists seldom exist and most paintings are more valuable when their creator has died. It's a human trait that we mourn the passing of something we took for granted and then elevate it to legendary status to live on forever. The Casino caught fire in 1981 and was demolished in 1982, much to the delight of the Wigan council members at the time, allegedly. Similar medical techniques are used to burn off warts. The rest of Britain was happy to bend with the wind and smile at Sir Terry Wogan singing the Floral Dance. David Soul was singing 'Silver Lady' and Tele Savalas gave us the most ridiculous song of all 'If.' You tube will verify that the world had gone completely off its rocker in the seventies. Kojak and Hutch, (part of detective duo Starsky and Hutch) two American TV stars hitting the top of the pop charts, really? I found salvation one evening in a local disco at a labour club. I knew from the minute I heard Little Anthony belt out 'Better Use Your Head,' that I'd been saved. I put the long division together that night. I'd heard 'Your Ready Now,' by 'Frankie Valli, when I was about thirteen and knew it was something different. Around the same time, I started playing my sisters brilliant collection of Motown records and they hypnotised me with their catchy lyrics and raw emotions. Like a christening I was baptised into the world of black American soul music. It stopped and started through my teens as new trends were marketed cleverly to grab my young easily influenced attention. But when that day or should I say evening came I was ready now. Ready to go on a pilgrimage that would last a lifetime. Little Anthony was calling me with the voice of an angel and preaching like a reverend preaching the gospel. He was telling me to 'use my head, don't be misled, think with your head, you will never find another love like me your whole life through.' *That is of course excluding my wife, I'm no fool she will read this*. At our local Labour club, I approached and asked a question to a brave soul who was up dancing on his own. Dancing in a way that I'd never seen before. His feet gliding effortlessly as he moved around the dance floor without a care in the world and with all eyes glued to this entertainer. 'Where do I go to hear this music and where do people dance like that, I asked this polished performer?' My questions were answered with gratitude almost as if he had found a long-lost friend and he lit my enthusiasm like a flame to a fuse paper. The place I was looking for was only eight miles from my home in Skelmersdale. The road to Wigan Casino was to be my equivalent of the Frank L Baum's novel 'The Wizard of Oz,' I was heading for the Emerald city. I wanted to meet the great and powerful DJ's of Northern Soul and so I set off courageously, with no brains but full of heart, along with my faithful friend 'Pricey.' Graham Price was a good mate who I'd known through school. He was into heavy rock and when we arrived at Wigan Casino for the first time, he was far from impressed. It was an early session, a seven to eleven Saturday night warm up before the actual all-nighter. A mixture of music was played, that varied between Northern Soul and the regular chart stuff of the day. It was an experience that confirmed my belief that there was more people who were like minded. They were dancing to records I'd never heard of before but the beat somehow felt familiar. My friend was keen to finish his pint of lager and go home to more familiar territory. That night I had arrived at a crossroads, as my friendship with Pricey was about to dissolve.

He wanted local pubs and local girls, I wanted a new music and a different world, and if I was lucky, girls too. On just one visit to the Casino I'd seen enough to convince me that the all-nighter was to be my natural progression. Strangely enough my first experience of the Casino and its tired and fading grandeur did not leave me awe struck. My second visit knocked my socks off and took my breath away. It was a week later that I decided to get the last bus out of Skelmersdale to Wigan on a Saturday night. This turned out to be a very good decision due to the fact that five or six people that I knew were waiting for the same bus. It was easy to strike up conversation with familiar faces. Some of these people I'd also known from school. As the bus winded its way through the town, more and more people heading for the Casino got on. Stop by stop a small gathering grew at the back of the bus, each with the same purpose and destination. It was too early for the drunks and too late for most other travellers. This green Ribble bus was as close as you could get to a privately hired coach. Over the years the drivers who worked the late Saturday and early Sunday mornings became accustomed to our unusual life style. One regular driver in particular managed to become somewhat of a hero, when he actually diverted from his normal route through Wigan town centre. He had spotted some trouble as we passed Wigan Wallgate station with what looked to be gangs of drunks fighting each other all over the road. He then drove right past our normal stop and took a right turn, down past the Wigan swimming baths and in to Station road, delivering us directly outside the doors of the Casino. I remember distinctly a woman who must have been in her sixties wearing a red head scarf complaining bitterly that it was not the right route. I look back and think 'that old driver he must have definitely had kids.' The bus journeys were as much a part of the night as the hours between twelve and eight. The conversation was totally Northern Soul, from the value of records down to what DJ was playing what sound. It was about who we knew and where they were from. It was about dancers, dance moves, spins and splits. When it was morning and we were back on the bus for the journey home the conversation was exactly the same but in reverse. Who we'd seen or met and from where. What new sound everybody was talking about and who sang it. What records did you buy and how much did they cost and then one by one we'd say our goodbyes for the week. We met as regular as clockwork for the next four years and in that time not one of us owned a car. Faces changed as new people joined the Saturday crew and others left never to return but the bus journey remained the same, a long but happy slog.

◆ ◆ ◆

CHAPTER 4

I've Got Something Good

The question my parents never asked was 'are you taking drugs?' Kind of upsetting really because I almost felt that I'd been looked upon as someone incapable of joining the ranks of James Dean. I thought I was a wild child, a young soul rebel as Stuart Cosgrove called us. But my parents obviously didn't see me that way. If you were to ask them about me, they would have probably replied, 'he likes to dance all night and he doesn't drink beer.' 'He sleeps mostly through all of Sunday and then goes to work all week.' The latter being the sad truth. I worked as a welder from the age of sixteen in a factory making steel pallets for the drugs industry. I was late most mornings and consequently in trouble most days. That's about as close to James Dean as I got. I soon came to realise that my life was now dominated by a clock which held up two fingers to me every day. I was a prisoner of time who was totally disinterested in the fact that I now had the skill to glue two pieces of metal together. I had left the confines of the school gates behind with a new-found freedom only to be forcefully enlisted in what could only be described as a prison full of bullies and burns. We had become a one parent family and my mother had woefully lectured me on the need to bring home a wage. With no family allowance given for anyone over the age of sixteen it was a case of earn or leave. An idol threat I'm sure from my mother's tongue, but I was not prepared to take that risk and therefore marched from factory to factory looking for gainful employment. I was considerably lucky to be offered a job as a labourer in a local factory, that was created as a cooperative. I never understood what that term meant, but they paid me a good wage for carrying huge steel pipes on my feeble shoulders on to a steel saw. I was strong but not well built and I worked alongside a brute of a man, who could probably carry me and all the pipes on his shoulders at the same time. After some expensive bribery, I managed to get one of the lads to teach me how to weld and eventually worked my way on to a line of welders. Being fast and nimble I was soon spotted as someone who could go near to the end of the production line and therefore gained a very good salary increase. My mother was of course happy to take my keep and I was happy with the remainder. My mother and father had an on and off relationship through the years and my dad was sent packing on many occasions. They couldn't get along but god knows they tried. The upshot of this was, food could be scarce in our house at times. My younger brother and I lived on powdered milk and jam sandwiches and occasionally we had treats like sugar puffs and proper milk. My mum's survival instinct was all about being shrewd with money, she had to be. She would ask both me and my brother what jam we liked, black currant and strawberry we would reply as she set off to the shop. On her return, we would be given mixed fruit jam and a brown whole meal loaf. Her clever ploy worked because it lasted longer and food went further. To save on heating we used to go to my grandfather's flat around the corner for a bath. I think the rest of the neighbourhood thought I was an aspiring Olympic swimmer as we lived quite close to the Nye Bevan public baths. I had no thought for embarrassment during those early teenage days and happily walked out of the front door with a towel rolled, under my arm. The good wage that I was acquiring made my Saturday nights that much more comfortable. I could afford the bus and the entrance fee to the Casino quite easily and what's more I could afford to buy a few records. Not only would I be able to add more records to my growing collection but also treat myself to something that resembled coffee in a polystyrene cup along with a pie of which I never questioned its contents. They said it was meat and potato and I believed them. If there was another version of Sweeney Todd in the basement of the Casino I would not have been surprised. Maybe that's why membership declined? The Casino coffee was something I will always remember. I can actually see myself holding this red hot volcanic steaming brown liquid and thinking it was bloody marvellous. Not exactly Starbucks, as you had to add your own milk and sugar which was in abundance in a sticky sludge spilt recklessly all over the counter. Very often, people who knew you went the Casino would ask 'what's it all about, what's the attraction?' They would feel knowledgeable by saying 'Northern Soul, isn't that 'Skiing in the Snow and 'Footsie?' The annoying part is, you can't actually deny this to people who also use 'under my thumb,' to condemn you even further. You have little choice but to agree and accept the sniggering. But what if you were asked by someone who genuinely wanted to understand the legitimacy of Norther Soul. How would you reply? What is it about Northern Soul that makes it so difficult to be categorised as easily as other genres of music? Country and western certainly sticks out a mile as does heavy rock, reggae and punk which are far easier to describe. Put any one of these genres of music on the radio and people would instantly identify with it. Country singers have that drawl to their voice that you'd recognise anywhere. However, play to a crowd of listeners, 'Can't help loving you' by Paul Anka and suddenly the 'please file under 'Northern Soul', becomes barely justifiable. Paul Anka certainly didn't intend this marvellous tune along with the equally well received 'When We Get There,' to be associated with a Lancashire club on the other side of the Atlantic. Here lies the first commandment, you don't need to be black to be a soul singer. Some of the most appreciated and well-loved songs on the scene came from some very unlikely sources. Michael McDonald formerly of the Doobie Brothers gave us 'God Knows,' a great one off soulful dancer. Kiki Dee's 'Magic Carpet Ride,' and

Bobby Goldsboro's, 'Too Many People,' were massive hits at the Casino. These well-known singers along with dozens of other white singers helped create a flip side to Northern Soul which is tentatively labelled as Blue-Eyed Soul. Sadly, along with the earlier mentioned Skiing in the Snow, we have to tell the truth and shame the devil, when it comes to being honest. The following records should carry a Northern Soul health warning on their labels. They have caused bitterness and many disputes amongst Northern fans and they have also helped stain the credibility of Northern Soul to the outside world. Who played the theme music to Joe 90? Which DJ wants to take ownership of that one? 'Nine Times Out of Ten, The Joker Went Wild, I'm Going to Share it with you.' The list of garbage played at the Casino is quite extensive. My immediate thoughts have always been, who made the decision to play them and in some cases, try to release them to the general public? Which Northern Soul DJ's sold their soul and took us from 'Turning Your Heartbeat Up,' MVP'S, to 'When Love Grows Cold, 'Ron Grainer Orchestra. Yet, regretfully there are some who follow the scene who will happily own up to them being a favourite. There's even a CD that goes by the title 'Guilty Pleasures,' which is designed around the fact that some of these tunes just get under your skin. You will be familiar with Doris Troy's 'I'll Do Anything,' and instantly allow it to be part of the imaginary approved Northern Soul play list. I remember clearly that the same title by Tony Blackburn covered as Lenny Gamble also getting a welcome reception. Tony Blackburn also had a record called 'Its Only Love' which also got a spin at the Casino. It was dreadful, but some liked it and even danced to it. The biggest sinner is the person who played it and there were plenty of those type of records to choose from. 'Wait a Minute,' Tim Tam and The Turn Ons, certainly living up to that criteria. Any group who called themselves by this name was never going to produce anything worth listening to. Stop for a second and imagine this groups member discussing what name to go by. 'Well my names Tim and your names Tam, and the rest of the group can be called the

Turn On's. Let's go with that, it's better than 'Temptations.' But rest assured someone has got it in a cardboard sleeve and actually treasures it. So, thank you Mr DJ for creating a complex situation that covers us in glory for the rare and exclusive music in our massive and exclusive play list. But try as we might we can't shake off the stigma associated with the Snake, or the Wigan Joker and the question remains, who played this vinyl garbage that labelled us as musically inept to outsiders? We didn't need too much help did we? We wore forty inch flared trousers, 'Spencer's,' and we sewed on badges to clothes and bags like a proud Cub Scout. Our attire also had a long leather coat that wouldn't have been out of place in the Gestapo's catalogue for spring and autumn. The girls on the scene are remembered for their full circle skirts and their light-footed dancing actions. They would spin skilfully like a ballerina on the big open dance floor and their skirts would rise gracefully to an angle that would put you in mind of a child's spinning top. Those dancers around them would afford them the room needed, it was customary. On a dance floor that sometimes seemed to be tilted unusually in the favour of more blokes than women, it was a welcome sight. Today I feel that we are still plagued with some of those awful records but we are also branded with misrepresentation by the jerk from the Casino time travellers club. Somewhere parked behind a new venue is a DeLorean, and its owner is in search of 1978. It's not the 'Enchantment Under the Sea Dance,' they're looking for. No, they're looking for the eternal youth dance that they feel is just a spray of talc away. They refuse to let go of the past and sometimes at certain venues you can't help but cringe as the blast from the past takes to the dance floor. I certainly believe in the freedom of expression and people have a right to be different. However, when a fifty-five-year-old bloke walks past me clapping like a toy monkey with cymbals and sporting a pair of red braces and Spencer's, I want the ground to swallow me up. I actually want the ground to swallow him up and then spit him out in to the year 2017. This white socked Time Lord has jumped through a worm hole from the seventies, clad in a sweaty vest and a display of mother's sewn on badges, telling me to 'keep the faith.' I will keep the faith by all means but I don't need to be told this by a lost cause trying to find one. Worse still is the moment they tell you, they wish they could have gone to the Casino. What the flux, capacitor is that all about? If it wasn't for the music you'd take thirty pieces of silver and deny that you ever knew the Casino. The question that I find possibly the strangest of all is, how can you go from Dobie Gray to Marvin Gaye and end up with Bobby Goldsboro all under the one roof. It can be easy to see the link from Marvin Gaye to the Northern Soul sound. From Marvin, we get a dynamic up-tempo Motown beat and a selection of songs that fit the bill. 'Ain't that peculiar,' has a quick pulsating piano rhythm right through from start to finish, which only enhances Marvin's rich vocals. The lesser known 'This Love Starved Heart of Mine, 'sounds tailor made for the Northern Soul scene and yet it wasn't a hit for Gaye and Motown. Dobie Gray's 'in Crowd' and 'Out on the floor,' are classics and will be appreciated for many years to come. Bobby Goldsboro was a massive success in the sixties with hit records such as 'Honey, 'even hosting his own TV show. For the Northern Soul scene, this white American, almost country style singer gave us 'It's Too Late,' 'Too Many People,' 'Longer Than Forever,' and 'She Chased Me,' all played at some point at the Casino. Another strange feature of the demographics of Northern Soul is its ability to breathe life back into the long forgotten. Many of the artists who have contributed songs to the turntables of an all-nighter, had disappeared into obscurity along with their demo records. Their loss of possible fame and fortune was to the benefit of the Northern Soul fraternity. Thankfully we were given the job of resurrecting and appreciating the vocals that had historically fell on deaf ears. For some reason, their demonstration record that was handed over to local radio stations, failed to get the attention it deserved. Consigned to the nearest dust bin or a tea chest at the back of a record shop, it would sit for years, until discovered by the keen ear of a collector or a DJ who recognised its potential. This rule was not just reserved for the struggling artist, it also applied to the stars of the day. Many well-established singers and groups released tracks that also failed miserably and would be quickly replaced by something that would hopefully project that artist back in to favour with the public. There were great Motown singers who also cut records that must have failed the famous voting council conducted by Berry Gordy. With all due respect a Motown loser was a Northern Soul winner. Records like 'You're Gonna Love My Baby,' Barbara McNair and 'When I'm Gone,' Brenda Holloway, were Motown gold at the Casino and none more so than Frank Wilsons Do I Love You.' It is fair to say it lives in its legendary status for all the right reasons. Berry Gordy gave Frank Wilson the option to carry on singing or stick to what Gordy thought best which was writing and producing. Wilson took Gordy's advice and continued writing and producing. The fact that this extremely rare piece of vinyl happens to have an irresistible melody only adds to its mystique. The price tag for the original only adds further status to what is the holy grail of some collectors. Rarity has always captured the collector's imagination, and it doesn't always have to be about the quality of the sound that sets it apart. Collectors of Northern Soul will relish certain labels and where one person's collection may be full of classic tunes another's will be crammed with rare sounds and obscure labels. At the back of the Casino one would find many sellers with boxes of vinyl records lined up side by side awaiting their eager customers. Tables awash with wooden boxes crammed with cardboard sleeves lovingly labelled with pride by their owners. Behind each table there where queues of would be buyers fighting for space and moving their fingers through tightly organised rows of records. Money moved quickly and from midnight until two a.m. the back of the Casino looked like a cross between a market place and Wall Street. The hustle and bustle normally subsided after two hours and the record dealers and buyers both disappeared into another part of the building. Some wealthier for their business some richer for their ownership. The night was then swallowed up by rituals, meetings, relationships and of course dancing. Peering over the edge of the balcony you could soak up the atmosphere and feel the heat of youth, vibrant in its prime, you then realised 'I've got something good.

Newspaper cutting from Daily Star January 22nd, 2001

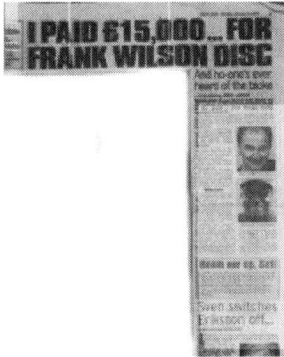

Music mad Kenny Burrell has blown his life savings on the most expensive single in the world- even though hardly anyone's heard it. The double-glazing salesman splashed £15,000 on the obscure sixties soul track Do I Love You, by little - known American artist Frank Wilson, at an auction. The single is more valuable than any releases by The Beatles, Elvis Presley, or the Rolling Stones because only six copies were made. In fact, Kenny's is the only known copy left in the world – and he won't part with it for any price. He's even turned down a £30,000 offer from Frank Wilson himself. Part-time soul DJ Kenny said 'Even he hasn't got a copy and he was desperate to buy mine. He offered me a fortune, but there's no way I'd ever part with it.

Moonlight Music and You

Classic

'I told him he could sing it to himself for free any time he
wanted! Some people may think I'm mad to spend such a lot
on a record they've never heard of, but it's a classic. "It's the
holy grail in soul circles. To own it is a dream come true. Despite the records value, Kenny of Edinburgh, plays it regularly as
he tours Britain as a DJ. He said, "it fills the dance floor every
time." Frank who went on to produce for legends including The
Supremes, Marvin Gaye and Diana Ross, said; "I was unaware this
record still existed. A Motown boss ordered all the masters to
be destroyed. "Somehow, a copy surfaced in England. I consider
it one of my life's great achievements."

◆ ◆ ◆

CHAPTER 5

I'm Where It's At

Long before it was known as Wigan Casino the dance hall now steeped in history was originally named The Empress. The 'Emp' as it was affectionately known to the locals of the town was built by the Atherton brothers in 1916. Their father was a boiled sweet manufacturer who had obviously made a substantial living, back in 1888. The Empress opened its doors for the

first time on November the 1st 1916. Awaiting its patrons was a lavish interior, complemented by 71 feet by 54 feet dance floor. Around the upper edge of this dance floor sat a spectator's gallery and a supper room. By 1926 some further refurbishment had taken place and a new annexe was built called the Pala is de dance. The building was possibly as far removed from anything that its name was supposed to portrait but there was no denying its grandeur. Its lavish interior was adorned with intricate carvings, some from wood and some from plaster. The sweeping balcony was also decorated in ornate curls that looked down on the people below mirroring their steps across the dance floor. The stage that joined both ends of the balcony was host to many entertainers over the years, from the big band sounds of Bill Blackledge in the fifties right through to the Rolling Stones of the sixties. The Empress held black tie balls for large companies such as Heinz and Courtaulds. Wigan police also held balls there too and in some way continued to do so until its closure. The list of well-known personalities who played the Casino is remarkable and to its credit very diverse. I often wonder how much the likes of Conway Twitty and Shirley Bassey enjoyed playing to those Wigan punters on a cold rainy Saturday night. Apparently, Shirley insisted on a new pink toilet being fitted back stage before she would accept the gig. She did have a song called 'My Body is More Important than My Mind.' I wonder if this is where she sat and penned it. The 'Palais de dance' changed its name around 1957 to Mr M's and it became used as a cabaret bar. By August 1966 the Empress had also undergone some further refurbishment and had now changed its name to the Casino. Over the following decades the building was used for some other unusual events such as roller skating and wrestling matches. It was also used to hold parties for poor children prior to the Second World War. By the time the Casino became host to the all-nighters it was clearly in a poor condition. It had seen better days and if you took a good hard look in the cold light of day, you could see the cracks of time bursting through its brick work. It was around 1977 that the Casino which had seen better days, began to live under the constant threat of demolition. Some people actually thought it would fall down by its own accord. My own recollection is somewhat blurred with compassion. I believed I was inside a solid old building and the only thing that would cause it to crumble was the vibrating vibrations coming from within. The Casino was no oil painting and through the dimly lit lighting the most prevalent colour was black. It seemed that everything was painted black. The doors the stairs, the seating areas all looked as if they had been dipped in oil. While strobe lights spun and flashed their way around alcohol infused night clubs, the Casino lit up its members with a pair of strip lights. Never had light created a better effect. Almost reminiscent of an American speak easy where the emphasis was on low profile, the dull glow created an almost secretive ambience. It worked impressively to allow the music to take centre stage and not to be outshone by any smoke and mirrors. Alongside the dance floor at certain intervals there were large hexagonal columns that majestically supported the balcony. Attached to each of these columns were mirrors that were always lost under a mist of condensation by the early hours of the morning. That condensation also dripped from the ceiling on to the mass of sweating bodies below. It was like rain drops falling on a fire as the heaving crescendo on the maple wooden floor reached boiling point. The dark brown wooden chairs and red topped Formica tables were built to last and not for style. The Casino was a simple design with sets of stairs in all four corners of the building. These stairs lead to the balcony which also had a bar area directly above the ground floor bar but was seldom open. In the corner of the balcony area was a small café sized counter, were tea, coffee and a meat pie could be purchased. The staff who patiently served these culinary delights seemed to do so with an easy friendly smile. They were the same faces week in week out and never seemed to change. They were to me at the time, middle aged women who either loved being up all night, loved Norther Soul, or just got well paid. I'd probably go for the latter. I always imagined Ma Woods as she was affectionately known as being their commander. Fearless and fast she took no messing as she collected the money at the main entrance under the watchful eye of the bouncers. Like a referee her word was final and she could designate that you should be evicted on the spot. She could scan you like an airport detector and in the blink of an eye know your age. No excuse was accepted for not producing a membership although generally speaking there was always someone outside who had a spare one to loan a desperate fellow soulie. I've seen Hilda Woods in some old film footage and she comes across as a very nice and a knowledgeable person with a sense of humour too. She knew her job and she did it well but she also had a hidden compassionate nature too. Tough and stern as Hilda seemed, she often showed that compassion over and over again when it came to a friend of mine. Steve Rivers was sixteen and as dedicated to the Northern Soul scene as any one you'd care to meet. He travelled to the Casino with his heart in his mouth as he was never sure he'd get up those stairs at the first attempt. Sometimes he was lucky and with the swathing notorious crush he would get past Hilda Woods with a quick flash of his membership and a pass of the exact money with no change required. However, on many occasions he was spotted by those eagle eyes and turned away and back in to the cold. She never asked him his age, she would just shout 'not old enough, out,' and that was all it needed. We were a little older than Steve and we would glance backwards with a pitiful shrug and only hope that he would get in later. This happened more often than not, I can't tell you how he did it, but by around one thirty he would come bouncing over to us with a massive grin saying, 'they felt sorry for me and let me in again and said don't come back next week.' Steve being told not to come back next week went on for months and eventually they gave up. For this alone he should be given the title 'brave Soul.' Such was Steve's passion for the music that he would make his journey knowing that his night would be longer on the outside and shorter compared to others on the inside. As we queued against the wall leading up to the large double doors, many strange incidents occurred that stay with me to this day. I recall three lads standing in front of the huge crowd beckoning any would be challengers to a fight. From their accents, I would say they were local lads who were probably pissed and had that feeling of invincibility, as you do. They surely never considered the odds and the fact they were looking to take on an army of very fit sober people who were ready to perform high kicks and splits and fast spins for eight hours solid. They looked like the bandits in the magnificent seven threatening the meek villagers. Suddenly those big black Casino doors burst open and from behind them came two familiar faces. It was like Hilda Woods had released the hounds of hell as we were given a public display as to why they worked the doors. They moved quickly, you never see doormen run, do you? They didn't kick or punch they just grappled two of the taunting drunks and moved them down the street towards the Ritz cinema before telling them to fuck off before they get damaged. I remember this situation clearly, as for some reason I felt like I had a couple of big brothers who wasn't going to let anyone touch their family. Another very similar occasion involved pulling up outside the Casino doors in a taxi. I could afford a taxi in later years and if you'd missed the last bus there was little choice but to hire one. Sometimes we'd get one between four, however the preferred transport would always be the bus. This particular night as the taxi driver pulled up outside the Casino doors there was a scene resembling a battlefield. All the doormen seemed to have been called in to action. There were bodies being hurled about all across station road and people running in all directions. I could see Casino members were involved just from the way they were dressed but again it would seem local lads had come looking for some trouble. The taxi driver and I stared at each other as these bodies crashed in to his car and rolled across his bonnet. He told me not to get out, like I needed to be told. We both watched in disbelief, until this Wild West carnage eventually fizzled out and I took the decision to open the taxi door and walk to the Casino door that was all of about two yards away. I could see the dints in this poor drivers bonnet and one of his wipers was now comically pointing to the road in front of him. There was the odd fracas over the years and yes it was occasionally with each other. I related this to arguments over drugs between either friends or suppliers. Money and bags of contraband swapped hands quietly but openly under the watchful eye of an interested crowd. I guess it was almost an advert for those looking to buy what was commonly known as gear. You could see who had just

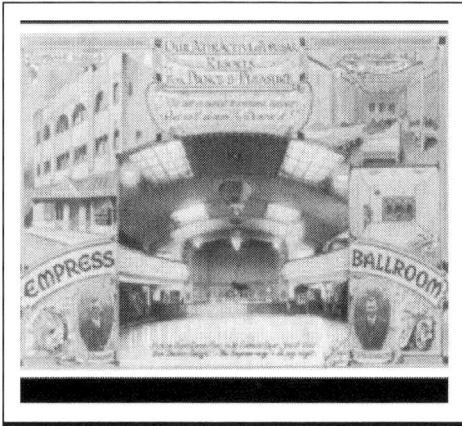

picked up a delivery and it would be easier for those people to deal drugs in a dark recess of the Casino than it would to take a chance with the law outside. The Casino created legendary stories from its revellers as it became a legend in its own right. But tragedy needed to strike first. The Casino wasn't a personality who could die in a car crash like James Dean or crash into a lake like the plane carrying Otis Reading.

But just like Joan of Arc she went to her death smothered in flames. The Empress of Wigan left behind a legacy that has managed to live on through generations. On the 16th of March 1982, a fire mysteriously swept through the building, severely damaging its structure and so condemning the building to be demolished. The Casino had been earmarked by Wigan Council for a new development which included a Civic Centre for a proposed cost of twelve million pounds. The council allegedly had no intention of renewing its license and therefore inevitably helped spawn a host of conspiracy theories as to the origins of the fire.

❖ ❖ ❖

CHAPTER 6

Build Your House on a Strong Foundation

To create a timeline to pinpoint the roots of Northern Soul would be nigh impossible. It would certainly not be out of the question to consider gospel as being the source to its beginnings. This religious music was designed to lift the soul and elevate the spirit towards god through the medium of music. The lyrics cried out for sinners to repent and rejoice in a new-found freedom alongside the rhythm of dance. The deep meaningful harmonies from these elite gospel singers and choirs inspired the next generation to take the music towards a new direction. The development of recording studios with eager new talent writing and composing new material began to change the sound of Soul forever. The fifties brought about a plethora of artists and groups that were destined to become world famous. Legendary songs were released from 'Sitting in the Dock of the Bay' to 'Mustang Sally.' Otis Redding, Wilson Picket and Benny King were story telling about broken hearts and lost loves while blues men were singing about no shoes, no love and lost harvests. Having Soul meant losing everything, losing your wife, your dog and your house in a fire. This mantle was later handed over to the country and western singer who added jumping off bridges, divorce and alcoholism. Not necessarily in that order. In 1872 a group of gospel singers from America reportedly sang for queen Victoria and it is said she was supposed to have wept for joy. Not a bad achievement for someone who is mostly remembered for saying 'we are not amused.' She was so impressed by their musical talent that she had them all stuffed and placed in the Albert museum. Actually, she had a portrait of them commissioned which now hangs in the New York Public Library. In the late fifties and early sixties record producers would scour churches looking for would be Soul singers. Up and down America gospel singers were being offered the chance to make a record that could possibly change their lives forever. Many of these singers were deeply religious and remained true to the church and wouldn't even consider the offer. Those that took that chance were very often destined to fail. But this wasn't always the case, every so often the record company men struck gold. Those golden vocals belonged to people like Aretha Franklin, Al Green and probably the greatest of them all Sam Cooke. The outstanding Cooke belonged to a gospel quartet called 'The Soul Stirrers.' During a concert in Los Angeles he was noticed by a 'Speciality Records,' A & R man Robert Blackwell. He had watched how the handsome Cooke had drawn a large number of young fans towards the front of the stage. After a lot of persuasion Cooke eventually signed for Speciality records. There were a few flops before Cooke found the right song which propelled him to stardom 'You Send Me.' Selling over two and a half million records, Cooke was now on his way to achieving legendary status. Women idolised Cooke, some gospel singers could see the type of fame and fortune now being acquired. Other gospel singers would not forgive his desertion of the church. Bobby Womack who was a guitarist for Cooke once said, 'I was afraid to make the change, the gospel world could be very scary.' The feeling in the gospel community was very strong and even Womack's parents rejected him for abandoning gospel. It wasn't until his father's final years that he finally accepted his sons chosen path. Bobby was reported to have said to his father, 'we just wouldn't have had the money to bury you dad if I hadn't of gone in to pop.' Aretha Franklin grew up in Detroit on the fringes of the city's east side ghetto. It was here that Aretha found herself growing up in the company of other kids who were destined for fame. Diana Ross, Smokey Robinson and all of the Four Tops lived in her neighbourhood. Aretha didn't have a happy childhood her mother deserted the family when she was aged just six. Her mother then died four years later. By the time of her eighteenth birthday Aretha had managed to be under contract to Columbia records. She didn't see this as a successful relationship and managed to negotiate a move to the Atlantic label. Although under contract, Aretha stated that the material she was being given at Columbia wasn't getting her anywhere. Almost immediately after her arrival she began to work with Jerry Wexler who had spotted what was missing from her music. Being a producer at Atlantic, Jerry sat Aretha down to a piano and gave her the strongest R & B backing group that Memphis could offer. To this end Aretha came up with some of the greatest hits that have ever come out on vinyl, proving beyond doubt that she was to be the queen of Soul for the next decade and beyond. Northern Soul owes a lot to gospel in many ways. There are many records on the scene that are from former gospel singers who for one reason or another didn't follow the same fortunate path as Aretha or Sam Cooke. Some famous singers emerged from a group background. Wilson Picket left The Valentines to find fame and David Ruffin moved on from the Dixie Nightingales on the same quest. This scenario is no different today as a member of a band is encouraged to go solo. Trying to make a connection between Northern Soul and gospel is never easy. The best example I can give is Levi Jackson's 'This Beautiful Day,' and the fact it is still played *religiously* at many Northern Soul gigs to this day. Follow that with Marie Knights 'That's No Way to Treat a Girl,' and suddenly your surrounded with the gospel sound. Marie Knight faded away from the recording scene and ended up as a telephone operator in Brooklyn. Before leaving her singing career behind she also left us with 'You Lie So Well,' as a follow up to her first and more popular recording.

◆ ◆ ◆

CHAPTER 7

Mr Creator

Mike Walker was the son of an entertainments manager who moved from Carlisle to Wigan when he was aged fifteen. Mike was employed by the ABC Cinema for four years as an assistant manager. One of Mikes favourite memories of that era was the night The Supremes, Marvin Gaye and Stevie Wonder, plus a host of other Motown stars appeared together on one bill. The amazing thing was the fact that they played to only half a house. That was in 1964 and not long after Mike found himself working in Manchester, where he became a member of the Twisted Wheel. It was here that his imagination became fuelled for the things that where to come at Wigan some time later. Mike returned to Wigan where he was offered a job as a DJ in the Beachcomber bar by Gerry Marshal. From the Beachcomber Mike progressed to be the DJ in the main hall of the Casino. Eventually Mike became the manager of the Casino and Gerry Marshal became the owner. Russ Winstanley was a DJ that was building a great reputation for his regular Soul nights at venues like the Rugby club and the Newtown British Legion. Mike and Russ came across each other at Russ's record stall situated in Wigan Market. Mike would buy records at the store and eventually they became firm friends. During this time, the Casino was losing customers to the Torch all-nighters in Stoke. It was Russ Winstanley who suggested that they should try a one-off all-nighter at the Casino. Gerry Marshal gave the go ahead and on September 23rd, 1973 the legendary Wigan Casino was born.

The Wigan Observer newspaper took some interest in the Casino and reported on certain major events connected to the Casino. Covering the good and the bad side of the all-nighters, this well respected local newspaper never took sides. Much to its credit you will see that it remained neutral in its approach and lived up to its very apt title. If anything, the Casino was portrayed in a good light and of course it helped it gain some free publicity. Throughout this book you will have the opportunity to read what was sporadically released through the years. I have re-written what is contained in these articles to enhance the poor condition of some of the microfiche that I managed to find. This first article is the writing of a journalist named John Gaskell from a column in the Observer called 'Grapevine.' Strangely ironic considering this was released on Friday September 28th, 1973. I was also drawn to some of the other stories that were situated opposite to the main feature. It shows that forty-four years ago people were stealing steak from the butchers and you could pay monthly instalments for a black and white TV. The first newspaper article I found was entitled '**Fans Flock to all night disco.**' Soul fans from all over the country, included one from New York flocked in to Wigan's Casino Club in the early hours of Sunday morning for the clubs first ever all-night Soul and blues disco. The only incident throughout the night was when two men were taken from the club suspected of possessing drugs. They are helping Wigan's CID with their enquiries. Organiser and DJ Russ Winstanley said afterwards that it was unfortunate because the event was such a great success. He said, 'it could have happened anywhere, in a youth club or a pub, it just happened to be here.' The police congratulated us on having a really well organised night with a well-behaved crowd, one policeman came back after he finished his duty to enjoy the music. One snag which Russ hopes won't happen again is that people had to come in once, show their membership card, go out and come back in again to show their cards once more. It was a legal tangle caused by the laws concerning Sunday entertainment, but the organisers think it's all been sorted now. They plan to run the all-nighters indefinitely but limiting the crowd to 800. Not many Wigan people attended according to one observer but the numbers were swelled by three coach loads of Soul fans from London, people from Scotland and Newquay.

Author; And we think health and safety along with bureaucracy has gone mad today. How on earth did they manage to get people to leave and then come back in again. Another startling fact was the turnout for the first all-nighter, eight hundred was surely unexpected. The three coach loads from Scotland and one from Newquay is nothing short of a miracle. The person who managed to get approximately one hundred and fifty Scots to travel down to Wigan for an opening night should have considered work in time share. Over the years the Scots were well represented and well received by the Casino, but to get so many on a debut as per the newspaper report is extraordinary. Maybe it was the warmer climate? Meanwhile we are also reliably informed that we had Soul fans from London and Newquay and New York. I would love to know who the New Yorker was and what he thought of Wigan as he made his way to the Casino staring up at the dizzy heights of the Ritz Cinema. Sadly, according to the writer not many people from Wigan attended. You would think if you had picked up the local paper and you lived in Wigan you would want to know what the hell brought someone from Scotland, Newquay and of all places New York to your town. As a local, I would be desperate to get inside just to see what was going on. But even years later just like the first account of the all-nighter stated, it never caught on completely with its home town, least of all its police and councillors.

◆ ◆ ◆

CHAPTER 8

This Could Be a Night to Remember

In direct contrast to the report of around eight hundred people attending its first night, I have read that a truer figure released by the Casino management as 634. This I feel, is probably a more realistic number. It also started at two o'clock in the morning after its earlier attendees had polished off their lagers and blue lagoons. These earlier revellers had possibly strut their stuff to tunes such as 'Rock the Boat,' Hues Corporation and 'Queen of Clubs,' K C and the Sunshine Band. Nineteen seventy-three would have seen them boogie on down to 'Lady Marmalade.' In the charts, there were albums by David Bowie, 'Hunky Dory,' and Roxy Music, 'For Your Pleasure.' Dad was probably talking to workmates about the IRA bombings in Manchester Victoria Station and London Oxford Street. There had been a terrible fire at the Summerland complex in the Isle of Man, which had claimed the lives of thirty people. This was all taking place the year we joined the European Economic Community. The events of mankind are created every day, yet history seems to have a peculiar habit of repeating itself or going full circle. As we surge towards Brexit I can't help but feel that the youth of today are losing their identity. Technology has a lot to answer for, as social media becomes the meeting place of minds. What would the vast majority of these youngsters make of their once youthful predecessors dancing through the night without a mobile phone or Facebook to capture the moment? According to social media and the comments that accompany some Casino footage on You Tube, 'jealous,' would be a description not too far out of place. I see statements like, 'I wish I'd have been there,' and 'You were so lucky back then.' God only knows how we managed without mobiles, I pads and Play-Stations. Record players and cassettes were the only way to play music back then and who would have thought that today you could put every record from every seller's box in the Casino on to one single phone? But this is what has helped add significance to the legend. Those grainy deep coloured Kodak photos and the muffled live tapes that captured that echoing DJ's voice. Posters and flyers along with original embroidered badges have made their way on to the collectors wish list. What was once just a vinyl collector's domain has now become a matter of anything associated with the Casino now carries a value. The anniversary badge that was given to punters free of charge every year has become very much in demand. It was not unusual to see these badges on the floor or discarded on a table by some people on the night of an anniversary. What's more I can only see these items increase in value as they become more and more difficult to find. While we were side stepping and dancing to our music, the three-day week was making life very difficult. Being at school I supported the three-day week and found it wasn't as bad as the news stations were telling us. The USA had withdrawn from Vietnam and Brezhnev and Nixon had signed a peace treaty to limit nuclear war. I was of an age that anything other than spots, music and football, never made the agenda. I almost became resigned to the fact that at some point someone would press the button and we'd all be blown to kingdom come. I recall seeing a government information television advert that mentioned taking the living room door off its hinges and placing it on an angle for the whole family to shelter under. The three-minute warning they called it, just enough time to boil an egg, before getting fried yourself. Don't look in to the light outside, otherwise you will be blind for the rest of your life, the remaining three minutes of it. Meanwhile dad goes into the kitchen cupboard to get the Phillips head screw driver to remove the living room door. Our doors where made of bomb proof hardboard and my dad wasn't exactly a handyman. When one of the legs broke off the settee he stacked a few Beano albums under it. Halfway through watching the Royal Variety Perform-ance the whole family would role in unison off the settee, as the 'Whizzer and Chips,' album slipped from its temporary support position. The peace treaty fell on deaf ears and never did reach some of those lads in Wigan. Those sporting collie flower ears liked nothing more than launching a mass attack on the late-night visitors to their town. Football hooliganism was rife in the seventies and it wasn't restricted to the big cities. Films like 'The Warriors,' 1979, told the story of a gang trying to survive being hunted down by rival gangs as they crossed the boroughs of New York. This had captured a massive audience of would be conscripts. We were living in the age were street gangs had de-veloped into many different guises. Skinheads were aggressive, Hells Angels were dangerous, football fans carried knives and Punks didn't care for society full stop. The streets were not safe and the police were no better. An investigation named 'Oper-ation Countryman,' had been set up to investigate large scale corruption from within the force. Eight officers were pros-ecuted but not convicted. It was said that over 250 police offi-cers were forced to resign and many faced further investigation and criminal charges. However, the results to these investiga-tions were never released to the public and therefore the link to the Masonic lodge inevitably gained credence. Were you to pick up the aforementioned gangs and drop them in another part of Europe at an England match, the rules suddenly changed. The seventies had an unwritten rule book that had paragraphs that said, 'it is your duty to join up with any other countrymen and knock the shit out of any person with a foreign accent.' The uni-form is optional, but a bald head and tattoos, preferably of a bulldog will help distinguish you from any potential foreign enemy. Remember that just because the Germans are singing a rendition of 'roll out the barrel,' it does not mean they are being friendly. It means that an attack is imminent and the French and Italians are ready to retreat at any given moment. After a night of free accommodation in a police cell it's time to return home with your new mates from London and Liverpool and then it's back to business as usual. Kicking the shit out of each other on a Friday and Saturday night, or, afternoon if attending a sporting venue. The Casino brought together a different type of person. No alcohol was served at the all-nighters and fighting was for those who ventured beyond the safety of Station road.

HEADLINE NEWS Wigan Observer Friday 1st April 1977

<u>**Attacked and robbed on night out**</u>

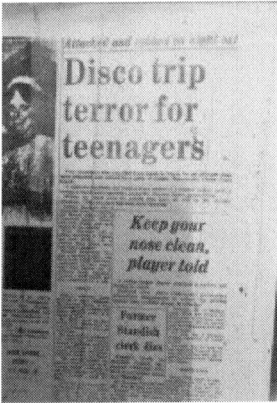

Disco trip terror for teenager. Four teenagers who travelled from Leeds to Wigan for an all-night disco were attacked and robbed by a gang of youths, Manchester Crown Court heard. In separate incidents, the victims were robbed of a leather jacket, cash, a medal, a watch and cigarettes, added Mr Randall Barker, prosecuting. Before the court were six youths who were all told by Mr Justice Crichton: 'This is a very bad case on all showing.' Anthony Sheridan (18) of Closebrook road, Pemberton and Ronald Taylor (18) of Drummond Square, Worsley Hall, both Wigan, were each gaoled for six months. Peter Pimblett (18) a soldier stationed at Chester and PAUL Shirley (19) of Jasmine Road, Wigan were both sent to Borstal. Kenneth Mitchinson (18) also a serving soldier was given a six-month gaol term suspended for two years, while John Davies (19) of Richards Road, Standish, received a three-month sentence suspended for a year. **GROUP** Shirley admitted being involved in three robberies, Sheridan and Taylor in two, Mitchinson in one robbery and Davies pleaded guilty to a charge of theft. Mr Baker said the four youths from Leeds had all come to Wigan for a disco last September. But they became separated and while one was walking through Wigan town centre he was attacked by a group of youths, including Mitchinson, Pimblett, Shirley and Taylor. 'He was surrounded, hit, punched and knocked to the ground, before managing to run away leaving his leather jacket behind,' said Mr Baker. After the attack members of the gang went to a public toilet to wait for other victims and came across the other three youths from Leeds, he added. **SEARCHED** They followed them into the toilets and one was asked for money. He was searched by Sheridan and his cigarettes were taken. Another Leeds youth was also struck, knocked down and kicked about the head and his watch was taken, while the fourth was ordered to hand over cash from his wallet and his St Christopher medal was torn from his neck. Mr Baker added when seen by police all the accused admitted their complicity in the robberies. Detective constable Leslie Burrows, in evidence, said Mitchinson, Taylor and Sheridan, were of previous good character, but Davies, Pimblett and Shirley all had previous convictions. Similar to the unwritten rule previously mentioned, a declaration of insurmountable friendliness was declared to be honoured within the Casino walls. In the book Soul Survivors, Tim Ashinbende from Stoke on Trent mentions that in all the time he attended the Casino he only ever witnessed two bouts of trouble. An educated guess would make me think that both Tim and I must have been in close proximity on one of those nights when for the first time in its history the Casino lights were suddenly and unexpectedly turned on. An announcement was made by Mike Walker that two people were posing as drug squad members and demanding cash and confiscating drugs from unsuspecting members. It would seem from what I could gather and from what I learned long after the event, they were pretending to be open to a bribe to drop charges and also pocketing any drugs. It was like a mugger holding a knife to another mugger. A clever ploy in my opinion and let's face it, the real drug squad didn't have much success over the years. These two characters and their scam had been discovered and all exits were quickly locked down. The hunt for the acting two was now on and those that had fallen for the scam, who by admission were guilty of possessing and taking drugs, were only too keen to point these fraudsters out. How this was brought to the management's attention and how these people had explained their predicament is almost unthinkable. But under the glare of the full lights of the Casino and accompanied by at least four large bow tied door men, they happily pointed them out. A moment I will never forget with regards to any other night at the Casino. I was sitting under the balcony at the rear of the Casino, just outside the record bar. A few friends and regular faces were now desperately shielding their eyes from the bright intense light which had never been seen after midnight before. Quick stepping across the dance floor in my direction there came what looked like a Blues Brothers tribute act. I could see fingers pointing in my direction and it felt like all eyes where upon me. Nervously I looked around me, if you could have played 'Turning My Heartbeat Up,' it would have been surreal. 'They think it's me,' I thought, I'm a dead ringer for who they're looking for I reckoned. Some speed freak is about to make a bad decision and get me pulverised. It turned out that the two guys they were after were sitting right behind me. They were wearing smart jackets that much I do recall as I watched them getting lifted effortlessly out of their chairs. They put up a slight defence in the form of a scuffle but they were no match for the heavy mob. Dragged towards the exit doors stumbling as if their legs could no longer take their weight, I watched in relief as they were launched head first through the doors towards the stairs. They took a few kicks on their way out too and I watched as a swarm of the friendliest people on earth bade for blood. Seconds later the lights went out and it was back to business as usual. For the evicted actors, it was a poor business decision that was never going to win them a BAFTA. Like the film of the same title 'Casino,' it played to different sub plots each Saturday to Sunday morning. Apart from the main event which was the music and the dancing, every other corner of the building threw up entertainment in various guises. Over the years I witnessed bizarre events that you were never likely to see at any other club. You could buy a pair of trousers, Spencer's, in a makeshift shop on the balcony corner before entering Mr M's. If you hadn't had time for a haircut that week you could get one in the hallway that run between the main room and Mr M's. This wasn't a permanent feature but I was shocked a few times to see two girls armed with clippers turning a good trade. More than once I watched a human pyramid being made in front of the stage and never quite got the reason as to why. It looked like a scene from Dumbo with a herd of elephants trying to create a structure that was destined to collapse on the poor souls at the bottom. The guy at the top risked life and limb as he clambered from shoulder to shoulder to get to the summit, only to come crashing down on to a solid maple floor. The one story that's been well documented over the years is the night someone reportedly took a short cut and jumped over the balcony to get to the dance floor. This was due to hearing Mike Post's, 'Afternoon on the Rhino,' and giving this person the feeling of being fully charged. Over the years I'd seen drinks, holdalls and even a bag of narcotics get launched over the balcony but never a human. There is another version of this story that I have read on the internet, on a page called 'The Sabotage Times,' in which an interview with Kev Roberts, mentions a similar story. He recalls playing 'World Without Sunshine, Sandra Philips and getting the same reaction. Another jumper from the balcony. Maybe this did happen on two separate occasions, but if I was going to jump off the balcony myself, it would have been to Ester Phillips and 'Catch Me I'm Falling.' How this person avoided landing on the many table and chairs below is a mystery in itself and the other question has to be, did he land on his feet? Lemmings, Rhinos and night owls, this was indeed the human zoo that brought together a cocktail of people, that has often been labelled as 'the strange world of northern Soul.' For all its traditions and determination to remain underground, there was one feature that constantly brought it into the public domain, 'drugs.' It was an inescapable headline that haunted the northern soul scene and the Casino throughout its existence. This darker side to the all-nighters provided ammunition and enough ugly press coverage to stir up tension between anyone remotely connected to the scene. For all its genuine purity and non-drug takers there was no hiding from its prevalence. It was ok to sing about 'sex and drugs and rock n roll,' (Ian Dury and the Blockheads) but in reality, drugs weren't to be glorified. In 1982, we were told to 'Pass the Dutchie on the left-hand side, by Musical Youth. The Beatles years earlier had made connotations to LSD with 'Lucy in the Sky with Diamonds and in later years Grandmaster Flash gave us 'White Lines.' As much as it was legal to make reference to illegal substances in musical lyrics, it was never going to be condoned as an acceptable activity behind closed doors after midnight. For the record, the Casino was not rife with drugs and so-called pushers, nor where there any giant busts like you see in the movies. The management made some effort to quell the use of drugs by making announcements every so often regarding not being tolerated. However, their pleas went unheeded and the small drugs trade continued unimpeded. Membership started to grow quickly and with it came more drug sellers and takers. It was inevitable that a place with an all-night low-lit atmosphere was going to attract the chancers, thieves and rogues who in many cases had no interest in the scene or its music. Before we roll down this avenue at great length, we must consider why that membership was growing and in what proportions. This next press cutting helps to substantiate how the Casino was being pitched and how it had become a magnet to those would-be entrepreneurs.

Wigan Observer date unknown

GRAPEVINE

If you're teetotal, tough as nails and Soul mad, join the queue before midnight

In my younger days, I was amongst the excited crowd surging forward to catch a glimpse of such heart-throbs as Jimmy Ruffin and Edwin Starr. But I have never seen Wigan Casino as packed as it was last Saturday night at the all-night Soul club. It is being widely acclaimed by Soul fanatics as the best thing since sliced bread (brown, of course). New Musical Express, described it as'...the country's top venue for Northern sounds...with a membership now standing at 20,000. In the August edition of Black Music, journalist, Dave Godin talks of its 'enviable reputation amongst the Soul fraternity' and describes its atmosphere as 'lively, cool and permissive. A leader in the field of Soul locations.' I just had to go and see for myself. **Wendy Worthington samples all-night Soul at Wigan Casino** Perhaps I should have been warned by looking at the number of people who were queuing outside at 11 p.m. (for a 2 a.m. start) But I was still staggered by the teeming mass of people inside. There were bodies standing, talking, walking, drinking (coke and milk only) and eating in every available place in the Casino. Only soft drinks are sold. Their astronomical prices ensured the bar was the emptiest, coolest place and you needed somewhere cool. I did wonder, while waiting outside for the great doors to this Mecca of Soul, why everyone seemed to be lugging suitcases and holdalls around with them. Once inside I discovered that a change of clothing was essential to retain any amount of comfort, in the tremendous heat created by jiving bodies. However, there was plenty of atmosphere created by the DJ's, Russ Winstanley from Wigan, Richard Searling of Bolton and Kev Roberts from Notts. **ENERGETIC** But even the energetic voices of the three DJ's could not penetrate my sub conscious enough for me to be able to differentiate between each record. I can honestly say, not being an avid follower of the Soul scene and having no wish to be re-educated having once experienced this night, I had never heard of any of these Soul sounds. But where they enjoying it, these Soul fans? Yes. The people I spoke to seemed full of the joys of spring at 3 a.m. in the morning. I asked one Wigan lad, 'do you actually enjoy this?' 'It's great he said, the normal Casino isn't a patch on this.' 'Don't you ever get tired?' I asked trying to reassure myself that I wasn't the only person in the place who wasn't absolutely delighted with the all-nighter. 'Well if I get tired I just put my head on a table and go to sleep for a bit,' he said. 'On a table?' I through sheer necessity, have slept in phone boxes – even in the ladies- but have never ever slept, from choice on a table, on a table. **LUSH BLOKE** I retreated hastily to the ladies only to hear snippets of conversation that went like this. 'It's great, why on earth didn't you tell me about it before?' 'Have you seen that lush bloke at the bottom of the stairs?' 'He looks like a right one.' Was I missing out on something? I stood on the balcony and watched people dancing...and dancing....and dancing....and dancing. Finally, I came to the conclusion that every one of those happy people in the Casino were Soul mad. So, I left them to it. I left them to dance, sleep on tables, buy 'all-nighter' badges, car stickers and Soul records. Yes, they certainly enjoy

themselves, these people. As no doubt do the Casino management. They have 800 – 1,100 people each paying one pound admission plus increased price on the monopoly of food and
drink, plus badges and stickers...well work that out. On September 21st, Soul fans will be able to celebrate the first birthday
of their club. Everyone entering will be given a special souvenir
and three hundred pounds worth of cassettes recorders will be
the special prizes at this. The all-nighters concrete proof of success night. So, folks, if you are mad about Soul, very fit and teetotal (or near enough) you go along to Wigan Casino's all-nighter
for a night to remember. You can forget your air bed, tables are
provided.

Author: Wendy Worthington's report certainly painted an unusual image of the all-nighter. I personally don't recall seeing
people with suitcases. However, given this was the year after
the Casino had opened and I never got my membership until
four years later, I won't say that her observations are incorrect.
I never found the drinks or food too expensive as described and
in a contradiction to her own writing Wendy Worthington says,
'people were eating all over the place.' One sentence says, 'with
the monopoly on food and drinks and 1,100 people in attendance, work that out.' As she says, one pound entrance, so I guess
£1,100 pounds. The food and drink, pies and coffees mainly
with bottles of coke, may have even pushed that over the
£2,500 mark. Taking into consideration, the staff and doormen
working over eight hours, plus DJ and management fees and of
course running costs. I would guess that the cash rich situation
being subtly suggested, was possibly quite far off the mark. I
once spoke to Harry Green in his office about the Casino's financial situation and he was very open and honest in his interpretation of the buildings welfare and dwindling membership. I was
involved in shooting some film footage for the BBC at the Casino
and part of the short documentary footage was of me and Harry
involved in a short interview regarding the Casino and its pre-

sent standing at that time. I think it got cut out of the final production, but I do remember Harry being open and honest and more than keen to answer any questions on the day. This was part of the youth programme called 'Something Else.' I had been approached to take part in this BBC 2 youth programme which combined social issues with appearances by pop groups of the day. Some footage of certain episodes is floating around on You Tube and it was looked upon with great affection by the teenagers of the seventies. There wasn't a lot of programming built around the youth and culture of the seventies apart from 'Top of The Pops,' and the 'Old Grey Whistle Test.' The latter being aimed at the older but cooler twenties age bracket. The footage of me and a group of friends at the Casino has been used on many programmes and the difference between the 'This England,' portrayal and the 'Something Else,' clips, is how modern the later filming looked in comparison, even though it's now well over thirty years old. I had been asked by a film director named Don Coutts and his producer Linda Cleeve, if I would take part and if I could think of anything that would be an interesting feature for the show. It was fortunate that a person I knew from school and also a member of the Casino had been chosen to be involved in the programme too. Mandy Knorr and I both suggested that there may be an interest in the Casino as it had faded from the public eye and its numbers had started to decline. I thought I was bringing some much-needed publicity to the Casino to help bring it back to its previous healthy state. Knowing what I know now, this is very much frowned upon, however it also proved to be helpful in the short term. I know this to be true, because for the next few months Harry Green would spot me outside at the door and ensured that I got in for free. Like any advertising on TV it prompted a burst of rejuvenation, which obviously swelled its numbers for a brief time, but it wasn't to be a cure. The director, producer and crew who were from London were totally amazed by the whole concept of the Casino and spent a few weekends researching the venue by attending the all-nighters for a few Saturday's prior to filming. On the day of filming Harry Green stood behind the decks playing 'Mr Floods Party, Compared to What,' over and over again, while a group of around twenty of us danced non-stop trying to recreate the atmosphere of an all-nighter in full swing. Vernon Ward, Bosey and big Mick as he was known, travelled down from Bradford along with Nigel Williams, Steve Rivers and Billy Sealey, who made the shorter journey from Skelmersdale. I felt that we made the Casino look more appealing in the way that we were dressed more conservatively compared to the past footage used in the 'This England,' documentary. Baggy jeans with a thin strand of coloured piping down the side and loose-fitting sweatshirts, were more in keeping with the street fashion of the time. Vests and forty inch trousers were long assigned to the bin marked 'did we really.' There were no badges, or white socks, or full circle skirts, we had moved on, which is more than I can say for some people on the scene today. I find it embarrassing to see men in their late fifties, even some in their mid-sixties looking like they've just been woken up from a coma that they slipped into back in 1974. Its 2017 and I'm with my wife at Blackpool tower ball room, staring at a pot-bellied, bald, fifty-five-year-old guy, bouncing around the dance floor. This painfully embarrassing throwback has the ability to be oblivious to the ridicule or the bewilderment of those around him. He is joined by the full circle skirted grandmother, who is desperately trying to relive her youth, but now looks more like Bette Davis in Whatever Happened to Baby Jane. I'm no kill joy, but is it any wonder that we struggle to be taken seriously. As you can see this gets to me and I promise that I won't touch on the subject any further throughout this book. The newspaper journalist struggled with the music and the mechanisms back in 1974. She wrote as if she was witnessing a strange cult and in some ways, she was. I'd like to suggest that not too much has changed since this article was written, we still hold the same values and the music has kept its vitality to this day. To the left of the main article there is a piece entitled **Theft Charge** It states the following. An unemployed labourer of Whelley, (Wigan borough) had the case against him adjourned at his own request at Wigan magistrates court last Thursday. He is charged with stealing one pound cash belonging to a Mr Herring on June the 9th. Bail was extended. Author: *It probably cost this desperate thief more money for a return ticket on the bus to get to court.*

❖ ❖ ❖

CHAPTER 9

Out On The Floor

Music, as we know, has had an amazing effect on humans since we first learned to walk upright. Throughout history man has felt the need to express his emotions through dance. It has been used to summon up spirits or bring much needed rain to a village in drought. The Great Plains Indians danced around fires performing sacred rituals to the beat and rhythm of a drum. Not too dissimilar to a hen party dancing around a heap of handbags on a Saturday night. Punk rockers pogoed to the Sex Pistols like Masai warriors in the heat of the African dessert. The similarities between cultures and dance are striking. Only our imagination limits us to what can be performed when it comes to dance, given that we have only two arms and two legs to work with. Dance can be defined as having the ability to express your inner emotions in unison to a rhythm. Most people can recall seeing a relative at a wedding who just loves to dance but seems to have no rhythm at all. Uncle Dave or auntie Sue, just can't keep up with the music. They're one step behind everybody else, and that step is usually on someone else's toes. I came across a perfect example of this one night or should I say morning, as I watched two couples enter through the exit doors by the stage. It was obvious these thirty somethings where there on the invitation of the doorman as I could see him direct them towards a chair and tables close to where I stood. Some of you may remember the sit com 'The Likely Lads,' starring James Bolam and Rodney Bewes as Terry Collier and Bob Ferris. The two men were something very similar to the sitcom duo dressed in their three-piece suits accompanied by two well dressed women. They sat smoking and staring at what they had probably been informed 'was a disco like no other.' The doorman who was a familiar face to me and always in our corner returned to his guests with four bottles of coke. It was obvious from their slightly uneven walk that they had no need for any more alcohol and coke was probably the best and only option. After a short amount of time, the two guys decided that this music was starting to stir their loins into action. They stood at the side of the dance floor, tapping their toes and carefully studying the dancers in front of them. Behind them came shouts of encouragement from their loved ones. Then it happened, a rush of blood and then the music hypnotically pulled them onto the dance floor. Out of control they went into something like the closing dance of the Morecambe and wise show. 'Bring me Sunshine,' was definitely not playing but these two guys decided to put in everything they had just seen in the previous half hour into one dance. I don't recall the tune but like the balcony jumper I mentioned earlier, this could well have been one of those 'Afternoon on The Rhino,' moments. They threw in a mixture of disco and salsa, all with the gusto that two pissed guys could muster. They came off that dance floor lathered in sweat, throwing their jackets to their chairs, like a boxer throwing in the towel and totally unaware of the show they'd just put on. These two guys had walked in wearing the worst suits money could buy. One was dressed in blue pinstripes and the other wore a light brown checked woollen design. They had the large customary lapels and the tight-fitting waist coats. Their trousers were flared and in all fairness, didn't look too much out of place. The guy in the brown suit got his breath back and decided that his initial attempts at dancing to Northern Soul still had room for improvement. I could see a slight argument breaking out as this man's girlfriend tried to pull him back to his chair by the arm. It was all in vein he was determined to hit the dance floor once more. With the amount of alcohol coursing through his veins hitting the dance floor would probably be with his face. I watched with some wicked malevolence thinking any moment now we are going to see someone flat line. I recall that he had now worked in a routine of side steps watching his own feet intently before looking up to see if he was mirroring the actions of those around him. The music stopped but he kept going, probably deep in concentration. Then of all the records that could possibly have come on it just happened to be Steve Karmen's, 'Breakaway.' This turned the dance floor into a thriving mass of high kicking and spinning bodies. Anyone who has been to the Casino and decided to go the toilet when this stomper was on can tell you that crossing the M6 on a unicycle would be easier than getting across the dance floor. The intense study and the Dutch courage, created a spark at some junction in this guy's brain and his inhibitions were set free to do as they please. He managed to pull off a child-like handstand that was not exactly all the way there. You know the type I mean, the one that's made by a four-year-old imitating his big sister while shouting 'look at me mummy.' He defied the laws of gravity making spins at 45 degree angles that looped back up to a vertical stance with the ease of a Russian acrobat. We tolerated his selfish liberty as he tried to execute the moves that those around him had practiced for years. Eventually his luck ran out and he found himself polishing the floor with his arse and his friend quickly came to his rescue. They laughed, but we didn't, not out loud anyway. It was something you never did to dancers who were not so light on their feet. It was okay to laugh at the good dancers if they slipped or crashed out of a spin losing their balance. They knew they were good and they were expected to try the difficult stuff. Northern Soul has some massive high energy songs in its catalogue and its interpretation comes with some pretty energetic movements. Yet, for all the up-tempo music that screamed out over those huge speakers there was also the slower deep ballads that helped you to catch your breath before the next hundred mile an hour stomper. Not only a welcome break for many but also a chance for the older members to grace the floor. No longer interested in throwing their spleen to the wind, these dancers often showed that there was a way to move that had more sweet soul rhythm than any fleet footed youngster could match. Dance crazes have been around through the decades, 'The Jerk, The Mash Potato, The Twist, The Locomotion, The Huckle-buck, to name but a few. Wigan Casino and specifically Northern Soul had some signature dances that set it apart. The common style of dancing was a simple step to the side and a drag back of the foot. Beginners can make it look a little like line dancing, but as confidence grows, more elaborate movements are added. This is where timing and picking up certain beats and breaks in the music allows you to clap in unison, spin, or go all out gymnast and put in the splits or a handstand. Strange as this may seem there are records that fit the bill for these energy sapping moves and there are many that don't. Another style of dance that was very popular was the shuffle and the stomp. Some people see the stomp as just a quickening of their normal routine with a bit more aggression and expression. The shuffle is a very fast skipping motion of the legs that is high energy and is similar to a boxer moving around the ring, a bit like Mohamed Ali in his prime. There is some old footage of Vaudeville dancers back in the nineteen thirties ('It can't last forever,' Columbia 1937 – Charles Bennett and Eugene Jackson) dancing in a very similar style to what was adopted at the Casino forty years later. The girls of the Casino had a style that complimented the lads with a more lighter step. A lot of the girls on the scene deliberately made an effort to put a more male style into their dance. With short cropped hair and smart pleated trousers, they created a style that showed they could match the lads not only in stamina but in great footwork too. Northern Soul has no hard and fast rules to how you move to it, it's not ballroom and it has no judges. Wigan produced some brilliant dancers through its years. The well-known Sandy Holt has been featured in many documentaries when looking back at the personalities who graced the scene. Vernon Ward was also a great dancer who could spin like a mini tornado. Winston, Sparky, Big Mick from Bradford all had a reputation for superb ability and dance technique. There were of course many more phenomenal dancers out there who were better known to their own close friends and local crowd. I spent a lot of time during my first months at the Casino watching in awe as these well-known dancers entertained like celebrities and set a standard for all to aspire to. I would sit at the balcony for hours and study their moves and wonder if I could do the same. The best dancers were those that added something different to the normal step and drag as I called it. These dancers occupied the top right-hand corner of the dance floor, right beneath the DJ. It was the corner of the dance floor where you would be afforded more room by other dancers. You worked your way from the back of the hall towards the stage, all the time knowing you had to up your game as you moved ever closer. Over the years some of these dancers would leave the Casino and inevitably made way for new faces to display their equally good moves like peacocks on a manor lawn. The very popular annual dancing competition had plenty of entrants. This took place on the stage in front of a huge audience and normally in qualifying groups of three. The judges were made up of members and management and the reaction from the crowd. I decided one year to enter and climbed up to the corner of the stage and gave my name in. I stood there nervous and apprehensive, watching the group of dancers who'd gone before me. I could see their every muscle tightening and the glaze of sweat profusely glistening under the light. They played to the audience with every ounce of energy they had. I realised quickly that this was not the time or the place to show the world my amateur footwork. Before Russ Winstanley could announce the next group of competitors, I had made my decision to disappear faster than a doughnut on a health farm allowing myself to be swallowed up by the crowd below, I left some poor bloke and a girl to fight it out in a gladiatorial best out of two. Hey, I gave them a fifty-fifty chance, which in some way was pretty decent of me. I will always remember the look on the lad's face when he realised that I'd done a runner and it was just him against a Scottish girl who'd arrived on a coach. Coming second to a person with fifty screaming compatriots surely wasn't all that bad. The competition was won by Sandy Holt in 1978, Sparky in 79 and Steve Caesar won the first one in 73. The prizes awarded were a hundred pounds cash one year and a moped another year. Other names that people recall winning were Danny Daniels 1975 and Simon O'Meily 1980. There was also Kim Habbits 74, Jethro 75 and finally Sharon Dyke 76. There is another item associated with the dancers of Northern Soul and it brings about some controversy in its own right. A fine white powder that is shared between dancers and can cause a lot of pain. Yes, were talking talcum powder, coke only came in bottles those days. This divine intervention that assists some dancers to slide gracefully across the floor is a scourge to many others. It's chucked around by some dancers like a baker putting icing sugar on a cake and as deadly as black ice on a pensioner's door step. The rest of us who can dance perfectly well without it have to put up with this artificial surface and risk breaking a leg for those who should take up ice skating and dance to Bolero if they want to slip around on a deadly surface. Rant nearly over, but ban it now before we all end up with a broken hip. Recently at a local Northern Soul charity night I watched some chap spray a bucket load over the floor which happened to be in front of the main doorway leading to the toilets. Marvellous, I thought, as I watched at least three people slide rapidly and uncontrollably through said door like they were being thrown out of a saloon in the old Wild West. Dancing is about skill and style, you don't see them throwing talc all over the floor at the ballet. Fred Astaire didn't say 'chuck a bit of talc down their Ginger,' did he? Ginger Rogers once said, 'if you think Fred Astaire was good, I did everything he did, but in high heels!' My point exactly Ginger, if I started spraying something sticky like, er, sticky stuff on the floor to stop me slipping and sliding, the talcum powder posse would be up in arms or under arms. So, I'd like to tell my own brethren to stick their talcum powder up their backsides where it will be more effect-ive to its true purpose. Meanwhile out on the floor, you will find the real beating heart of Northern Soul. The majestic and the magnificent. The people who came to dance and lose them-selves in that beat and rhythm. The sweetest feeling belongs to those who dance with nothing but air beneath their feet and a disregard for time.

HEADLINE NEWS

CASINO TRIO DANCE ON TOP OF THE POPS

Wigan Observer; Friday, December 6th, 1974

Three young people from Wigan appeared on Top of The Pops last night – dancing to Wayne Gibson's 'Under My Thumb,' after winning a dancing competition at Wigan Casino. The competition run by Wigan Casino and Pyle records involved practically all the dancers in the Casino on that Wednesday night and the three winners were Anne Rogers, 18 of Old Lane, Shevington. Tom Mercer, 18, of Pendennis Crescent, Hindley Green and Alan Rimmer, 18, of Leigh Street, Newton Le Willows. They went down to London on Wednesday and had lunch with Wayne Gibson and Nosmo King (of the Javells) before visiting Pye Records studio. At the studios, Anne, Tom and Allan, clapped for half an hour to provide the clapping bits on the Chosen Few's new record 'Footsee' which will be released in January in a Wigan Casino sleeve. The three winners wore Wigan Casino badges when they appeared on Top of The Pops.

Author; Nosmo King was of course the stage name of the Javells singer Stephen Jameson, taken from 'No smoking,' I've heard stories of how this name allegedly came in to being and I'm not entirely convinced of its accuracy. Apparently when trying to come up with a stage name Jameson spotted a 'no smoking,' sign in a hospital and after tweaking it a little came up with 'Nosmo King.' I loved this story when I first heard it, mainly because I'd failed to see the play on words initially. But the internet tells us that, H Vernon Watson was a variety act in the thirties who also went by the name 'Nosmo King.'

◆ ◆ ◆

'Beauty Is Only Skin Deep' – Temptations

HEADLINE NEWS

Search for Miss 'Wigan Casino.'

Wigan Observer, Friday, March 8th, 1974

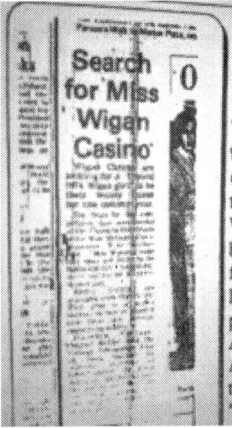

Wigan Casino are looking for a typical 1974 Wigan girl to be their beauty queen for the coming year. The heats for the competition start this Sunday at the Casino to the strains of the Malc McGuire Disco, Manager, Mike Walker said, 'Miss Wigan Casino 1974 doesn't have to be fantastically beautiful, were looking for a typical Wigan girl. Entry forms are available from the Casino. First prize is a holiday for two in Majorca and there are several runners up prize.

Author; So, from this article we can gather that a typical Wigan girl was not much of a looker in 1974. Fantastically beautiful, was too much to hope for by all accounts. It also shows that the Casino management were pretty generous when it came to the value of their prizes. A holiday for two to Majorca was a very good offer back then. There is no record of any winner or any other information regarding Miss Wigan Casino.

◆ ◆ ◆

CHAPTER 10

I'm a Peace-Loving Man

Apart from the influx of drugs, the next big concern for the Casino management would be trouble in the shape of violence. Had the wrong people got through the doors there would have been plenty of opportunity to cause massive amounts of problems. There were easy pickings for thieves with people's bags scattered all around the tables and piled up in corners. Toilets were checked regularly for drug use. Records were stolen from collectors and coats went missing by the early hours of the morning. Not wishing to paint the all-nighters in a bad light (that light was already bad enough and the paint as I've already said was black all over) but through the years I came across many dubious incidents. The saddest moment for me was when I bought my first long leather coat from a guy I worked with. Delighted with my second-hand fashion accessory, I was aware that they were always being stolen from the Casino week after week. After a little research, I was amazed to discover that a cloakroom existed in the lofts of the Casino. A narrow staircase leading up from the balcony, just after the tea bar. This lead to a busy queue waiting to deposit their coats and bags safely until the morning. Having paid a small fortune for this brown, full length leather coat I had no intentions of letting it disappear into some light-fingered persons wardrobe. I handed over my prized possession to a young lady at the serving hatch and in return received a raffle ticket. Isn't it strange how the fear of losing an expensive item transfers over to the fear of losing a piece of paper with a number on it? Clutching my ticket with no care for the number printed on it, I turned to notice a small recess that run like a channel hidden behind the staircase. Out of pure curiosity, I walked innocently into the poorly lit area. There seemed to be a small glow of red light that made visibility very difficult. It was here I had my first introduction to hard drugs. The look on my face would have resembled a startled child. I knew there were drugs in every corner of the Casino but I had never seen a syringe outside of a hospital before. Sitting on what looked like a church pew were at least four people. I could see a rolled-up sleeve and a needle hanging limply from the arm of a person who was now being transported to another world from its contents. I watched as the person sitting next to them removed the needle in a nonchalant way, as if to take ownership. I was not a presence to these people, I watched motionless as a thin red stream of blood squirted towards the opposite wall a few feet away. I turned away like I'd witnessed a murder through a key hole. I thought this only happened in the movies. I thought it was only in places like New York and Harlem and all those places stigmatised by film producers. I'd been watching Starsky and Hutch and Kojak arresting these people for years on end. My god, Wigan had people doing heroine? I struggled with this accidental awakening for some time and can still picture it clearly today. I never looked in that area again, I convinced myself it was a one off and that these people were chancers. They had in my mind discovered this sanctuary from a curious visit to the Casino and realised that it gave them a place to do their hard drugs unnoticed. From that day on I became far more aware of the complexity of the use of drugs at the Casino and from the following features you will see how it is difficult to defend or deny its prevalence. The trouble with drugs is the trouble it causes. There was nothing to fight or argue about in the Casino, as alcohol was not served behind its bars and therefore it lacked the fuel that ignited the punch ups that occurred at many other clubs. So how does a crowd of people who politely apologise for standing on each other toes on the dance floor become the scourge of the local police and the disdain of the local council? The simple answer is, some of that crowd broke into pharmacies. The following three articles could easily be entitled 'make sure you use contradiction.' This is exactly what the public perception of the Casino would have been, given the newspaper coverage of the time.

All-night gathering a hit with Soul fans

The all-night Soul gatherings at Wigan Casino is a great success. Soul brothers from all over the country arrive at the club on a Saturday night which has been acknowledged in special music magazines as the Soul night in the UK. Organiser Russ Winstanley, who masterminded the venture says that record sales in the club are going very well and there has been **no trouble** at all since the opening night. The success has even affected a newsagent's shop in Station road. Every Sunday morning the shop has a sales bonanza as hordes of hungry dancers make the long way home.

Bouncers in revenge attack

Three doormen at the Casino club, Wigan, who attacked a 21-year-old man inside the club causing injuries requiring sixteen stitches were ordered to pay him one hundred pounds compensation each for injuries by judge Bingham at Liverpool Crown Court.

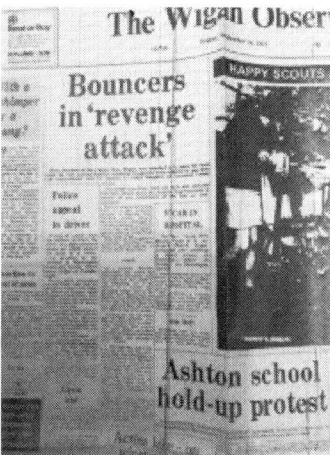

The judge also fined them twenty-four pounds each and directed that they should serve six months imprisonment in default of any instalment of the fine of compensation the men were Herbert Green, aged 41, a self-employed plumber, of Browning Road, Standish, Lower Ground. Michael Patrick Lyons, aged 21, a builder's labourer, of O'Brian Grove, Parr and John Barker, aged 38, a fitter of, Valiant Road, Marsh Green Wigan. They were all found guilty of unlawfully wounding Peter Brown, a general labourer, of Kendal Road, Higher Ince. Mr Norman Wooton, prosecuting, said Brown had intervened to stop Barker using too much force on a youth he was restraining and in the course of the scuffle that developed Barker went to the ground. Later Barker and the other two men attacked Brown in the toilet, beat him about the face with their fists and kicked him while he was on the ground. Imposing the fine the judge said he had seriously considered sending them to prison. 'Club doormen have exactly the same duties as other members of the public not to use unnecessary and excessive force,' he said. In this case they had a difficult job with only four doormen on duty and 1500 people on the premises but they had used excessive force

primarily for motives of revenge. He took into consideration that they were having their work cut out because the situation was one which could easily erupt if adequate steps were not taken to deal with the outbreaks of violence. The fact that Barkers position of doorman at the Casino Club had been jeopardised by having been seen on the ground could have caused provocation that made him act out of character.

Drug raiders on way to Casino

Three teenagers who stole nearly 3,000 tablets from a Wigan pharmacy were on their way back to Wigan Casino with them, when they were stopped by the police Wigan Magistrates were told on Tuesday. Scott Barrie, 18, a food processor, of Falkirk Grove, Norley Hall, Geraldine O'Brian, 17, unemployed, of Orchard House, Scholes, and a sixteen-year-old girl admitted burglary at a Wigan pharmacy Upper Dickinson street. (hidden paragraph) of tablets in a paper bag. In a statement to the police, Barrie said 'the two girls went into the shop and searched for the tablets after he forced open a door. It

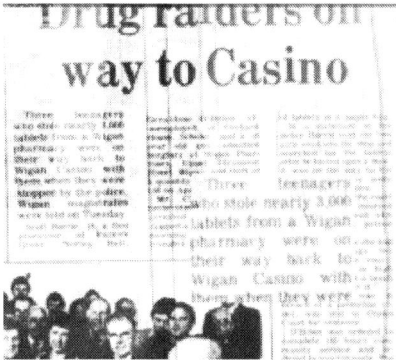

was on the way to (hidden paragraph) was in breach of probation order, was sent to Crown Court for sentence. O'Brian was ordered to complete 140 hours community service and ordered to pay £20 costs.

Author: From these articles, it would be easy to assume that the Casino was a haven for drugs and violence. Further newspaper articles from the Observer and other local newspapers may also help to substantiate that opinion. It would be important to keep in mind that thousands of loyal supporters gathered here every week sometimes twice a week and on balance the incidents that brought some bad publicity where seldom in comparison. 'Compared to What,' you may ask? Compared to the police presence required at other events. Other night clubs filled the accident and emergency rooms up and down the UK with late night fights and alcohol related injuries. Football hooligans needed escorting to and from matches for fear of gang rivalry and mass brawling. Drugs were not the sole property of the Casino they thrived in every town and city, which is no different to the clubs and bars of today. In my four years at the Casino I witnessed the police in attendance on two occasions. They walked around the balcony for half an hour, taking little interest in proceedings. Whatever their reason for visiting, they were not as imposing as perhaps they had intended. If anything, I would have assumed the management felt more uncomfortable. Once in the darkened recesses of the Casino there seemed a sense of anonymity by some drug pushers. Once past the doormen, there seemed a lack of authority, which meant a relaxed atmosphere. An invitation to deal to any would be takers. The presence of the drug squad was quickly transmitted from person to person and in a short time they would have noticed that all eyes were upon them. They did have some limited success and I remember watching as some people were taken out of the exit doors lifted, almost off the ground by their elbows. I also recall a friend of mine who thought it would be funny to get a group to huddle together while he passed out polo mints in a guilty fashion. He knew he was being observed and later told us of how he had to plead his innocence as he was dragged down the exit staircase. On a more serious note there were some alarming stories that revolved around certain drugs and their origin, more so their ingredients. Those in the know would mention that there were 'Back Street Bluey's,' circulating. I was told that this meant some back street amateur chemist was producing something as close to the original as possible but without the full ingredients. I was told that some of those ingredients included 'rat poison.' Apparently rat poison was the closest chemical to a vital ingredient needed to produce the desired effect. The newspapers continued to express the concerns from different quarters and therefore accusations backed with evidence was never far from the public eye.

❖ ❖ ❖

CHAPTER 11

Just a little misunderstanding

'Halos are for angels,' Blanche Carter would tell the Casino faithful. Those faithful working-class people spent most of their week earning a living. I spent my week working in a factory as a welder. Sometimes I'd work the Saturday morning for the extra cash. This meant trying to get some sleep later in the afternoon, having started work at 8am and working through until 12.30pm. The day dragged from Saturday afternoon onwards until the time came to walk to the bus stop or meet up with friends and travel by taxi to Wigan. Some people, when going on holiday feel that the holiday starts at the airport, others say it's at the destination. For me it wasn't the journey, nor was it arriving outside the building that was about to explode with the rarest Northern Soul sounds in the country. It was walking across the dance floor, putting my bag in its regular spot and just looking back at the whole room. It bristled with expectation and in the blink of an eye it suddenly delivered you into a better world. The working class were now in charge of freedom and expression. Having clocked in and out for the past five or six days and conformed to whatever governed your pay packet, this was pure liberation. But tiredness kills. Dancing from dusk till dawn needs energy. The music demanded your attention and each DJ had their own array of classic sounds that sapped your energy. Legs were drained of their strength and bodies lay strewn around the building trying to regain some stamina. By four am the heaving dance floor was beginning to show gaps, and patches of highly polished maple wood were reflected like a shimmering lake. Just when it seemed that the night was about to turn into a slow burner a record would reignite the whole atmosphere and once again the dance floor was lost beneath a sea of souls. It would stay that way until eight o clock. It had taken a brief rest. Maybe the DJ had tried to break a new sound, or was it just a record that only appealed to a few? Whatever it was that emptied the dance floor, it soon regained its numbers. DJ's had to break records, the scene depended on it and the crowd expected it. However, it could take a few weeks for a new tune to catch on, a DJ had to be prepared for an abandoned reception, until the record grew in popularity. Those dancers that were in need of a rest were obviously lacking one ingredient, 'amphetamine.' As you walked around the Casino's balcony there were various types of people who passed you. The clean person, who had a healthy respect for the music and the scene. The clean person was prepared to give up around 5am, slumber in a corner and then make a hard-fought effort to dance the last hour. Then there was the speed freak, wide eyed and chewing gum incessantly, happy to bend the ear of anyone who would listen. They had no desire to sit still for any other reason than a quick chat. They could hear music that was faultless and their veins coursed with highly charged emotions allowing them to draw on hidden reserves. They could dance with a high tempo until the music stopped at 8am. They also found it difficult to stop dancing between records. They didn't eat, they didn't even urinate, their bodily functions were going to take some time to regain some normality. For certain people the use of drugs at the Casino was purely in a recreational sense. For others, it became a catalyst that lead to a downward spiral into addiction or worse, death.

Headline News

Wigan Observer: Friday 3rd October 1975

All-nighter drugs probe Coroners pledge after girl 20 dies.

Allegations of drug trafficking at Wigan Casino's Saturday All-Nighter are to be investigated by a coroner following the tragic death of a 20-year-old Wigan girl. The promise came from central Cheshire Coroner John Hibbert at the inquest on unemployed shop assistant xxxx of Carr Lane Worsley Mesnes, held at Warrington last Friday. After hearing evidence Mr Hibbert said 'from what I have learned about the Casino at Wigan, I think this place needs a little bit of investigation. 'I will make my own enquiries about the Casino, I want to find out for myself,' he added. Xxxx was found dead in bed at a house in Avondale Drive, Widnes, on Monday morning, May 19. The cause of death according to Dr J.G Benstead, home office pathologist, was morphine poisoning. Dr Benstead, who has carried out a post mortem, told the Coroner there were a number of injection marks on the girls left forearms. Mr James Graham Webster said his daughter was a shop assistant until she came out of work.

The last time he saw her alive was on Sunday morning, May 18th, when she was with her friend xxxx in Market Square Wigan. **OVERDOSE** She was planning to go with xxxx to her own home in Bedford. Mr xxxx said that his daughter had been in good health although in December last year she entered hospital after a morphine overdose. This was the first time he hears of his daughter's association with drugs. In answer to the Coroner, Mr xxxx said he once had to visit Salford police station over his daughter. She had been attending the Casino club in Wigan and staying there throughout Saturday evening until the early hours of Sunday. He admitted that since December 1974 xxxx had had trouble with drugs. He and his wife had managed to get her to see a local doctor, who had said her home life 'could bring her round.' **OBJECTION** 'She used to go the all-nighter at Wigan despite our objections,' said Mr xxxx. 'Sometimes She would come home at 10am on the Sunday morning and even in the afternoon. She also travelled to places like Manchester.' P.C D Laithewaite said, 'at 7.35am on May 19 he visited a house in Avondale Drive, Widnes, where he saw the body of Miss xxxx fully clothed on a bed. There was a bruise mark on her left arm. Det Const A E Sharples of the drug squad of Cheshire Constabulary, said he visited the house and took away various items which were sent for analysis to the Forensic Science Laboratory near Preston. Questioned about the Casino Club at Wigan, Det, Const said it was believed drugs were passed there and there had been numerous arrests. But more information in regard to the Casino could only come from the drug squad operating in that particular, he said. Xxxx of Avondale Drive, Widnes, said he and his wife lived at the house but on May 17 they had an argument because she wanted to go to Wigan Casino. **PULSE** 'I did not want to go so I went to Salford for the weekend. When I came back on Monday morning I found miss xxxx in bed upstairs. 'She seemed to be alive.' A short time later my wife was shouting at xxxx and saying there was something wrong with her. I went over to see miss xxxx and I thought I detected a faint pulse. 'I tried to bring her round but could not do so.' Miss xxxx of Avondale Drive, Widnes, told the Coroner she met xxxx on the train when she was going to the Casino on the Saturday night. Mrs xxxx said that later after leaving the Casino, she returned home but Miss xxxx went off as though going to the bus station. 'She turned up at my house on the Sunday evening,' she said, 'she asks me if she could have an injection of morphine' and I agreed. 'I had one at the same time.' Then xxxx went to lie down. 'I took her a cup of tea later on and she seemed alright.

ACCIDENT The Coroner said he was satisfied xxxx had not intended to take her own life. 'I am satisfied this death was accidental through an overdose of morphine,' he said. 'From what I have learned about the Casino at Wigan I think this is a place that needs a little bit of investigation.' He said he would be getting in touch with the drug squad for the area, concerned particularly with regards to allegations of drug trafficking. They should take any steps they could to prevent similar deaths of this nature in the future he said. Mrs xxxx reminded the Coroner that she wrote a letter to the chief constable at Manchester just after her daughter had been taken to hospital about Christmas 1974. She reported in her letter what allegedly went on at the Casino and the chief constable replied that he would be looking into it. 'But the Casino is still open,' she said. 'I will make my own enquiries about the Casino- I want to find out for myself, 'said he Coroner. He recorded a verdict of accidental death.

❖ ❖ ❖

CHAPTER 12

Temptation Is Calling My Name

The Northern Soul scene was an open invitation for drug abuse if ever there was one. Some have said the percentage of people attending Wigan Casino and taking drugs was very few. To be fair many people who frequented the Casino were oblivious to the entire drug culture and took no interest. The simple fact was if you weren't interested you would never have noticed money changing hands. 'Guilty until proven innocent,' was allegedly the motto of the local constabulary of the day and a rather unfortunate incident helped me to understand exactly how this was applied. As I left the Casino one morning tired and incidentally drug free, I happened to lose my footing on the pavement edge. I was then followed by two keen eyed police officers who took hold of me by both my arms. They took me to a furniture shop that was only a few yards from the Casino and walked me into the recess that lead to the door. It was one of those shops that had a glass display frontage and it was in here that I was given two choices. The first choice was to strip and be searched for possession. Alternatively, I could opt to be taken to the local police station, where upon my parents would be informed that I was being held on suspicion of possessing and taking drugs. The last thing I needed was my parents to think they were about to take part in the Lancashire version of 'Midnight Express.' Therefore, I reluctantly agreed to strip. My bag was emptied in front of me and the contents examined piece by piece. They must have thought they were on to something when they came across a tennis ball sized plastic food bag that rolled out on to the floor. The closest they got to finding anything criminal was two sweaty socks that my mum insisted came home wrapped and only opened when entering the washing machine. The smell, she would say was deadly and even more pungent if I forgot to hand them over on a Sunday morning. Sometimes my bag would not be opened until the following week and if I'd left any sweaty clothes festering for the week, it could be as deadly as mustard gas. So, the socks in a bag were a house rule. As I stood confused, cold and nearly naked in my Ethel Austin underpants, I could see the sympathetic looks from passers-by. I was hoping that the long arm of the law wasn't going to stretch into my nether regions and that they would soon realise that my trip up had brought about their slip up. I was eventually set free and the only thing left on display was two thick wooden items, plus some cheap looking MDF furniture pieces. They may not have got their man on this occasion but I do recall these veritable blood hounds chasing someone around the balcony of the Casino one morning. They'd get within an inch of collaring their prey when all of a sudden, a bag would be launched over the balcony deliberately ripped open before doing so. The shower of pills would be quickly picked up by some eager grateful hands and the runner would be caught but not in possession. This may be an exaggerated tale but I was also informed that some people on recognising members of the drug squad, would deliberately approach them with tablets in their teeth and swallow them in defiance.

HEADLINE NEWS

Wigan Observer 24.10.1975

Sir – We are two girls who go to the Wigan Casino All-Nighter and we think it is about time someone put in a few good words instead of bad words about the place. We understand the reason for all the bad publicity but think of all the thousands of people who would be disappointed if the Casino was closed down just for the sake of a few drugs and the few people who take them. We also think that if the Casino was closed it wouldn't solve the drugs problem because the people who take drugs would find another Soul club to go to and find drugs there. We understand the feelings of families of people who have died from drugs and we sympathise with them. This letter is not only for our benefit but for the benefit of thousands of Soul fans from all over the world. As for the two boys giving evidence about the Casino, this is our advice. 'If you don't like the Casino, stay away, no one is making you go.' For Northern Soul fans, there is not another place in the world as good as the Casino All-Nighter.

Yours etc.

Two Northern Soul fans – Linda and Chez.

Author; An admirable attempt to defend the Casino by Linda and Chez, but you really wouldn't want these two to represent you in court. Telling the newspaper 'if you close the Casino, drug takers would find another Soul club to go to,' may not have helped the cause. Poor choice of words here Linda and Chez, because your defence strategy for the All-Nighter is not helping. Basically, you are saying there is a drug problem and it only happens at Soul clubs. Sympathising with those families who lost 'people,' who have died from drugs, also lacks sincerity. The actual sign off *'yours etc.,'* may well be the initials to their protest group, 'End the Casino.' Not sure by this account whose side these budding journalists were on? The accusations regarding the Casinos darker side were to continue until its doors finally closed. If ever a story was needed for a newspaper column, a stroll down Station road by any hack worth his salt, would get results. Between the hollow threats of closure aimed at the All-Nighters, the vinyl managed to keep spinning week after week and so did its revellers. In truth, it was a game of publicity chess that inevitably ended with a check mate and a checkout in mind. The land sitting beneath the corner stones of the Casino was earmarked long before it was turned into the shopping centre it now occupies.

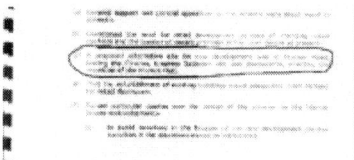

The correspondence shown here was discovered when I was making my initial research during the mid-eighties. Searching through any documentation I could find in the Wigan library, I came across this scant evidence of future planning. It reads as follows.

(A) General support and general opposition to the scheme was about equal in strength.

(B) Questioned the need for retail development in view of changing retail methods and the number of vacant premises in the town centre at present.

(C) A proposed alternative site for new development was at Station Road linking the Cinema, Empress Ballroom site and Woolworths, enabling the retention of the Market Hall.

(D) That the refurbishment of existing buildings would adequately meet demand for retail floor space.

(E) Raised particular queries over the design of the scheme for the Market Square redevelopment.

    (i)   to avoid monotony in the facades of the new development greater variation in the elevations should be introduced.

Q.8. LEISURE FACILITIES

The G.M.C highway proposals have substantial repercussions on leisure facilities in the town centre. Many of the premises are owned by the council and their replacement is essential. They could be replaced by either a purpose built cultural centre close to the central area or by the conversion redevelopment of vacant premises on the edge of the town centre which would you prefer. Cultural Centre – Vacant Premises – Other.......

In addition, the Queens Hall and Wigan Casino are effected in the plans. Do you think the council should replace these facilities currently available at these premises at its expense? Yes – No.

Author; Although I cannot provide an accurate date to these papers it is painfully obvious that the councils intentions were very clear. Fast forward thirty years and not only do we have a shopping centre but a café and a wall display featuring the very spot discussed in item C. Those with a keen eye may also have noticed that item (D) is nowhere to be seen. Item (D) seems to have been removed and I'll leave that omission to any budding conspiracy theorists that may be out there. Could it be (D) We propose that this building is demolished by any means possible? Not exactly the X files, not even worthy of investigation because it transpired long after the nighters were all over. Those people who are involved with the future planning and development of towns and cities have a job to do. The end of the Casino was inevitable and if there were some mysterious circumstances surrounding its end, we are richer for it.

CHAPTER 13

Let Me Make You Happy

A more appropriate title to this section would have been 'Last night a DJ saved my life,' (Indeep 1982 R&B) but sadly wrong genre. The DJ's of the Casino were seen as the lords of the turntables. They were responsible for stitching together the rich tapestry of music that created the very footprint of the scene. Those footprints were then stamped in approval across the dance floor. Their part of the agreement was to bring their faithful audience a legacy of music that was only for the purists and built to last. It had to be right and it needed to fall into the category listed under, 'think.' Not many people would describe 'Northern Soul,' as a thinking type of music, but this can be proven quite easily. Interplay, Derek and Ray, I Go to Pieces, Gerri Granger and 'I Don' t want to Discuss It, Little Richard. If from those records you can think of anything that links the three together, then you certainly have a musical ear. If you are familiar with these records, you would know that one sounds historical with its harpsichord lead and the other being a slow romantic ballad. The Little Richard track, is a quick paced dancer, with Soul going through its grooves like the letters through a bar of rock. Yet all three have captured their place in the hearts and minds of Northern Soul fans for all time. The variation in the music allows its followers to argue over what is and what isn't a classic. The DJ's didn't follow any hard and fast rules, they followed their gut feelings. They made a decision and played what their instincts said could be a floor filler. Breaking a record took a calculated risk, an empty dance floor could be disastrous. Getting a reputation for emptying the floor was not the best CV for a Northern Soul DJ, especially when you were playing the best gig possible. But new sounds were vital for rejuvenation and longevity. Russ Winstanley in my opinion was sometimes given less credit than he deserved. The greatest era of our famous all-nighters was very much down to his determination and vision. The love he had for the music was without question. The question that was sometimes asked was, 'did he try to cash in on the scene?' Russ actually had a record kiosk in the Casino for some time and I bought my first record from this small entrepreneurial shop. At the top left-hand side of the balcony I gave Russ, two pounds for Rain with Charity Brown's, 'Out of My Mind.' It seems I must have been out of my mind, because it was an awful record that my friend had recommended. Russ had seen a niche market and supplied to that demand, which was no different from recognising the Casino's initial potential. Russ was first and foremost a DJ and I think that we should remember this when discussing his contribution to the all-nighters and to the pages of Northern Soul history. Russ had the responsibility of getting the night off to a good start and being the first spot behind the decks. He played to the crowd and knew how to build up the atmosphere. I never recall him straying too far away from the classics and he also liked to inject a bit of personality between records. Some DJ's stuck to announcing record titles and the artists in a robotic monotone drawl. Russ would inject a bit of news or tell us who was making an appearance at the Casino with regards to live artists every now and again. Signature records for Russ was the outstanding Dutch Robinson, 'Can't Get Along Without You, 'or Sergio Mendes and as he would say 'the girl with no name, for 'Love Music.' He has appeared on many interviews reminiscing on the history of the Casino and it is, because of this, I feel that some have frowned upon his genuine commitment to Northern Soul, beyond the Casino. The commercial release of the albums entitled 'Casino Classics,' founded by Russ Winstanley was also another string for this astute business minded DJ. The records that made up its play list however, would not be deemed as classics by many Northern Soul fans. With some poor covers of original classics and Tony Blackburn singing as Lenny Gamble, is it any wonder that Russ gets the cold shoulder from his peers occasionally. Following Russ at the decks was the very popular Richard Searling. Highly respected and well liked, this down to earth DJ was incredibly popular and still is to this day. When Russ brought Richard on board it was like a premier football team getting a star player. He knew his audience and he also knew that remaining faithful to the concept of Northern Soul was a matter of principle. That principle relied on good judgement and not succumbing to what some other DJ's played as a quick fix. Searling as far as I recall did not play 'Joe 90' or 'The Joker Went Wild,' I may of course be wrong. It is, in my own opinion, that I believe his playlist stayed close to the rare and dignified as possible. From my years at the all-nighters I find it difficult to pin the tail on the donkey. In other words, I can't say which ass played 'Love Hustle, Nine Times Out of Ten, or Wait a Minute,' Tim Tam and the Turn Ons.' As easy as I can associate certain records with certain DJ's, with Richard I am forever reminded of 'Eddie Hollman's, Where I'm Not Wanted.' I also have a quiet admiration for Richards attempts to move the music into a new direction at a time when the scene was beginning to lose prominence. Playing 'Let's Spend Some Time Together, Larry Houston,' 1980, was in my opinion a game changer. It woke people up all over the Casino like an alarm clock to a more modern Soul sound. Larry and Richard were the equivalent of Williams and Watson, they were telling us all, it was 'Too Late.' Too late to turn the clock back and too late to stop the infestation that was commercialism. Somewhere between 'Skiing in The Snow, Wigan's Ovation,' and It Really Hurts Me Girl, The Carstairs, an opportunity to grab a piece of the cash machine suddenly came to the fore. Labels such as Pye, Spark and Destiny, burst on to the scene like an avalanche of vinyl gold. This provided genuine soul fans the opportunity to own what would have been an expensive cover up. The famous 'cover up,' was yet another quirk that added to the collector's misery. The announcement of a new record with a fake title and a fake artist was part of the game called exclusivity. The DJ who broke a record that went big and created demand had something that allowed them to be wanted and needed. A fever would break out amongst collectors to be the first to find the real identity of the covered record, which was normally a white piece of paper over the real label. Elusive records could generate a keen following and eventually the owner of that record could also demand a good price for the wisely stored supply of copies kept in readiness. Famous cover ups included Frank Wilson's 'Do I Love You, under the pseudonym of Eddie Foster. 'Can't Help Loving You,' was covered as Johnny Caswell before being outed as Paul Anka. The DJ's worked the floor and kept us coming back for those rare and in demand sounds. The line-up became established and you could set your watch by the arrival of certain jocks on stage. Brian Rae was the regular six o'clock shift and for me 'Many's a Slip,' was another signature tune that graced his presence. Brian was a great crowd pleaser and he could keep you on your toes all night. Before Brian you would get a few guest turns and the line-up could vary from week to week. In the middle hours DJ's such as Pat Brady, Kev Whittle, Keith Minshull or Soul Sam where responsible for keeping the temperature rising. Meeting Soul Sam recently at the Grand Hotel Llandudno in 2016, I was eager to ask this former teacher a burning question. I had remembered Sam playing an instrumental that had grabbed our attention back in the days of the Casino. Covered as 'Night Time Shadows, by Theodore Light-foot and his Orchestra,' I had later learned that it was actually the right title but the artists where called 'Gang Band.' I asked Sam if he still had it and he duly obliged by digging it out of his record box and presented it to me and a Llandudno DJ by the name of Dave Chapman. Asking the price, I was astonished to hear the reply of five hundred pounds. Far be it from me to put a price tag on any record, but after hearing it again on 'You Tube,' I couldn't help thinking that this was a cover up of Rolf Harris and his Stylophone. It may also be more of a collector's item these days. Keith Minshull was a DJ whom every time I saw him, seemed to have a permanent scowling expression. It made me feel that unless you were introduced to him personally, then best left alone. We never spoke. But I have read that he has a massive fan base and when I came across a page mentioning that he had been unwell back in 2011, I saw nothing but kind hearted well wishes from many of his friends. Keith has probably got one of the best CV's on the scene and he is also credited with getting The Torch off the ground in 1970. Keith Minshull for all his history and knowledge was in my opinion a chancer when it came to spinning something obscure at the Casino. I have a faint recollection that Keith played 'This is the House Where Love Died, by Patti Brooke's,' which incidentally received a good reception. It is however as close to disco as you can afford to be and with the likes of 'Brainstorm's, Loving Is Really My Game,' getting the same welcome, it also signalled the massive swing taking place by the eighties. As you can see, I'm not interested in defining or lovingly reminiscing about the music that we all know really well. I'm taking it for granted that most readers would put 'Mel Brit, or Frankie Beverly on a completely different level to 'Let's Make Love, Ronnie Love.' Fact; Russ Winstanley gave out hundreds of free copies of 'I'm Gonna Share It with You, Diana Foster,' we took out our lighters and moulded them into ash trays. Was this vandalism a stand against the tirade of the tailor-made garbage that was being thrown at the faithful? Returning back to the fictitious court case where Northern Soul is on trial, I would instruct my barrister to ask the following questions. I'd like to ask each of the 'Lords of the Turntables,' if they could be called to give evidence, 'which one of you played, 'It's Only Love,' Tony Blackburn?' Who is responsible for 'Lost Summer Love?' Who on earth said, 'I'll play 'My Hearts Symphony?' More importantly, if you were the disciples of Northern Soul and were sent forth to spread the faith, what Judas played Hawaii 5 -0? For Christ sake, it couldn't get worse. The only thing worse than the deranged DJ who was putting this on the turntables was the empty head who was dancing to it. It was written with crashing sixty foot waves in mind and twenty natives paddling the fuck out of a canoe by the Ventures 1968. They also composed the theme tune to the American detective series 'Police Woman,' just in case you're looking for something new to play at a venue somewhere near you. At the same time, I am reminded by the sensible half of my marriage that many avid Northern Soul fans would tell me to get of my high horse and tell me it's a matter of personal choice. As mentioned earlier, it gives us license to argue all day long over what is a guilty pleasure and what is an out and out classic. Another excellent DJ was the suave Dave Evison. Approachable and knowledgeable, Dave was often seen strutting his stuff across the dance floor and looked as comfortable dancing to the music as playing it. He was the only DJ I ever saw dancing, so he gets some extra credit. When behind the decks at Wigan he had the ultimate job of sending us home tired and happy. Before getting to the last three records of the night he would mix it up like no other. Being part of the crowd who stood and danced at the corner nearest to the decks, we had probably become familiar faces to Dave. The smiling Dave Evison would tolerate requests and at one point allowed the crowd from Skelmersdale to pick a number one record for the week. 'All We Need Is Time for Love,' and 'Burning Spear,' by 'Soulful Strings,' were two that we pushed Dave to play at the time. It was nothing serious or permanent, because Dave Evison was another DJ who kept it as close to the mainstream as possible. Dave did play George Benson's, 'On Broadway,' it was a twelve-inch version that had a long intro and again very much signified the changes in music and tastes. A funky R and B slow burner that was a million miles away from George (Bad) Bensons, high tempo 'Supership.' Dave was also responsible for another important hallmark for the Casino and that was the highly significant 'three before eight.' It became legendary in the way that people can identify famous pieces of music with films or soaps. The haunting theme to the 'Godfather' or the brassy introduction to 'Coronation Street,' provide a lifetime ownership of the music that is instantly associated with their introduction. In the same way, the three before eight has become synonymous with Wigan Casino. They were played in a specific order, starting with 'Long After Tonight Is All Over, Jimmy Radcliffe,' a slow romantic ballad. Solid vocals and lyrics that could be played at the end of any venue, were couples could embrace and turn slowly, lovingly lost in time. Except that was not the intention at the Casino and so for many it was a sit-down song. The next in line was 'Time Will Pass You By, Tobi Legend. Talk about a lesson in not wasting time, this certainly spelled it out to you with a climbing Heart rendering crescendo. The lyrics were written by a guy called John Rhys from the UK, who knew nothing of the records history until 1982. Bessie Grace from Alabama aka Tobi Legend, told us 'all you have to do is live for now,' and 'life was just a 'precious moment.' I would guess that most of us never really heeded those wise words back then, but now those words are starting to resonate strongly for many of us. The last record of the night, or morning, whichever you prefer, was the appropriately entitled 'I'm On My Way.' This Dean Parish tune was perfect to signal everyone's departure and its haunting melody and lyrics meant it has never felt over played. I have read accounts that to many, this was their least favourite of the three. As a matter of preference, I think the Radcliffe song is the strongest of the three. Once more we encounter the age-old debate that will live on forever with Northern Soul followers. This has to be the strongest of the three or why else would it be the last to be played? There we go, argument won. Released on the Laurie label in 1970 in the UK, then later re-released in 1975 and again in 1978 as a Casino Classics EP (extended play- incorporating more tracks than the normal single 45). Reaching number 38 in the UK charts during 1975, slightly tarnishes its membership to the underground world of Northern Soul. However, it's history will ensure that it lives on as long as people still go to all-nighters. Many DJ's find it hard to break with tradition and still end the night with 'I'm On My Way,' possibly jogging the last memories of Wigan Casino and that thrill of being young and slightly rebellious.

HEADLINE NEWS

Half million reasons for saying thanks Russ

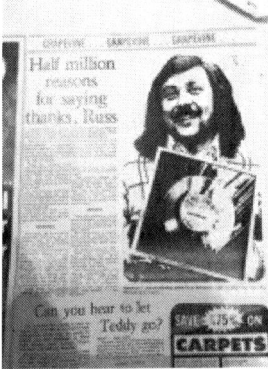

Trying to pick the next hit record of 1975 is as difficult as trying to pick the winner of the Grand National. There are no real certainties and plenty fall at the first fence. But last year a record company asked two Wigan DJ's to do just that and recommended ten of the top Northern Soul sounds that were likely contenders for a place in the charts. And so 'Goodbye Nothing to Say,' by the Javells and Wayne Gibson's 'Under My Thumb,' were released. The rest is history. Those ten numbers that Russ Winstanley and Richard

Searling tipped have sold over half a million copies between them. And Pye records dismal performance in singles during 1974 perked up in the last month. So, last Saturday night Pye records said, 'thank you,' with a surprise presentation to Russ of a silver disc for his help in establishing the 'Disco Demand,' series of records. Now there are many in the record business who reckon that 1975 is going to be the year for Northern Soul.

INCREDIBLE Russ says, 'as far as we're concerned 1974 was an incredible year for Northern Soul. It' difficult to imagine this year being better.' The vast amount of publicity received by Wigan Casino' s Soul all-nighter has established Russ as one of the top Soul DJ's in the country. More publicity seems certain to follow with BBC and ITV camera crews having filed documentary film on the club. In the next few weeks Russ and Richards ear for a hit will be tested when Pye release 'Footsee,' by Wigan's Chosen Few, coupled with 'Seven Days Too Long,' by Chuck Wood on their Disco Demand Label. The records release has been delayed while the initial pressing of 30,000 is altered. The name 'Chosen Few,' had to be altered to 'Wigan's Chosen Few,' because of an injunction threatened by a group of the same name. IMPORTS Russ has opened a record shop in Hallgate so now he can tune in to the demands of the record buying public as well as disco goers. He's specialising in imports from the USA including some singles by English groups such as 'Led Zep that were never released before. So, what's in store for 1975? Apart from re-releases by Paul Anka and Keith (remember 98.6) the kids are beginning to collect records just before their time. Old Beatles singles are making something of a comeback and take a deep breath there is a growing demand for the wholesome sound of the most artificial group ever known The Monkees.

❖ ❖ ❖

CHAPTER 14

People That's Why

People came from all over the country, which was obvious by the amount of coaches parked outside the Casino. Throughout the night DJ's announced records as requests from various cities and towns from every corner of the UK. 'This one goes out to the Bradford crew, Broadway Sissy.' 'Great to see the Carlisle crowd here tonight, Village of Tears.' It felt like the DJ's were saying 'thanks for coming.' Travelling members seemed to have their own meeting point in the same spot week after week. You could be walking from one end of the dance floor to the other and pick up on many strong dialects sitting in groups, around tables and chairs or huddled together in one corner. Scottish, Welsh, Geordie, Scouse, it was a melting pot of cities, towns and strong accents creating friendships that were to last for years. When the Skelmersdale crowd first started to frequent the Casino, we could be found seated at the very back in a dark and gloomy recess under the stairs. Unlike Harry Potter we were there by choice and the only dark forces present was the huge mass of people that congregated across the dance floor. We were there because stepping on to that dance floor for the first time would go largely unnoticed. No matter how much confidence you possessed, you were scared to death of that first dance, even after all your practice at home in front of the mirror. Most of us would have spent time watching the movements of the better dancers from the balcony and committing them to memory. At the back, you could merge into the crowd and take your first fleeting steps, ignoring the fact that you were supposed to be doing this to appreciate the rhythm of the music. Heart pumping with nervous uncontrollable legs you would look down at your feet and watch them step from side to side, clumsily standing on your neighbours toes every so often. Practice as they say makes perfect and as remarkable as it may sound, Skelmersdale had a group of dancers that had no intentions of taking a back seat. Time, it takes time, as the legendary Edwin star once said. And so, it was that after some time we moved location and were found seated further towards the central area of the vast dance floor. We had a new-found confidence and with that confidence came space. The middle part of the dance floor had the luxury of more room per dancer. It was here you were expected to be more extravagant and that extra room meant you were at the business end. Splits, spins, handstands and a whole lot more was possible in this area. There was more light afforded to the middle of the floor compared to the black hole of dark space at the back. Not exactly under the spotlight but certainly more visible. Those newcomers to the Casino would be looking down at you from the balcony with some expectation and watching someone go from a spin into a handstand or similar move would raise looks of admiration. The saying 'don't go into the light,' has been used as an expression of it being the pathway to accepting death. For those dancers at the Casino it had an extra line. 'Don't go into the light, unless your certain that you've paid you dues. The area of the dance floor positioned under the two fluorescent tubes and close to the stage demanded some showmanship along with agility. Like a Monopoly board, moving around the Casino and owning the top right-hand corner of the dance floor was like going from Old Kent Road to Park Lane. The best dancers gathered here and showed off their skills, watching people like Sandy Holt drop into a box splits in perfect time to the music was jaw dropping. He and many others like Vernon, took northern Soul dancing to the highest levels. Everyone remembers a great dancer who may not have shared the limelight, but there were so many. There is also a famous picture of a young girl performing the splits in mid-air. Used in so many posters her amazing pose is legendary and speaks volumes with regards to the acrobatic level of dancing. Alongside the dancers there were people who became well known for their opinions and involvement in keeping the scene in check. The enigmatic Pete Lawson gets a mention in many Northern Soul accounts as a highly respected but strongly opinionated character. Here's where I take a completely different avenue to those who have been deeply involved with the history making and documenting of the scene. Many Sunday mornings I travelled home on the bus sitting near or sometimes next to Pete and his good friend Clive. Sitting at the back of the bus to Ormskirk they talked quietly and seldom engaged in the general chatter that normally followed an all-nighter. On the few occasions, I did start up conversation with Pete, I found him to be polite yet secluded. Tolerant to those who had barely touched the scene, I almost felt he viewed me as a passer-by. He was renowned for his knowledge of Northern Soul and sadly I was unaware of this at the time. Only long after his death did I become aware of just how much he was respected on the scene. Some people would see Pete as shrewdly opinionated. He obviously suffered fools gladly because I do remember discussing certain records with him and his look of disapproval was almost too apparent for him to conceal. My conversation would be based on the here and now and what was big on the playlist of the day. Pete would stare at me and complain about the fact that I'd just said, 'I like that record by John Drevars, 'The Closer She Gets.' I'd then get a short lecture on the fact that I was allowing myself to accept any shite that was spoon fed to me, before he'd turn away and look out of the window for the rest of the journey home. I knew there was something different about Pete Lawson, but at the time I just thought of him as someone who had been on the scene longer than I had, nothing more. But it seemed that he had gained huge respect from all over the Northern Soul scene regarding his balanced views and genuine love of the music. I look back now and think of this as Simple Simon meeting the pie man, or the equivalent of a taxi driver with Lewis Hamilton in the back. My inadequate ability to talk in depth about records, history and labels must have pushed all the wrong buttons except the one marked as dick head. The only correct button I did push, was the one to stop the bus, near my home in Skelmersdale. The Ormskirk crowd continued on for another eight miles, probably grateful that the rowdier of the two towns had departed. Sadly, Pete Lawson passed away at an early age and I know from the experienced writings of Stuart Cosgrove in 'Young Soul Rebels,' that he was dearly missed by those who knew him. The complexity of life is often lost in the mundane requirements of living day to day. We wake eat and sleep with hardly a thought for our mortality. It's not until we are put in to precarious situation that we allow ourselves to become fearful of the possibility of death. From crossing the road to boarding a plane the natural instinct to remain safe will automatically kick in. Youth has a funny way of having a blatant disregard for the grim reaper. The exciting journey ahead for the young will outweigh any other risk factors. The rite of passage only comes with experience and that is why many of us in our more senior years will look back and see a road strewn with near misses. The temptation to seek out new experiences and dabble with drugs would come knocking firmly on the door of anyone who was spending the whole night dancing. Sometimes that door was a revolving door and it had a habit of spinning some young lives out of control. It seemed that someone always knew of a person who had lost their life to drugs. It was by no means prolific and it was news that generally came from that person's home town. I have a personal opinion that may be lost in translation but here goes. There were two types of drug takers who attended the Casino. Those that saw Saturday night as their one and only dalliance with speed and other narcotics. Then there was those who continued to abuse throughout the week. I met the latter on a few occasions and was lucky enough to be able to frown upon their extra use of drugs and found it simply pointless. But drugs have a way of gripping people tightly and not letting go. Further stories would continue to tarnish the already darkened reputation of Wigan Casino. The newspapers picked up on the beleaguered parents who were obviously heartbroken and pointed to the fact that their son or daughter had attended the Casino. Who could deny them pointing the finger as they searched for answers and somewhere to lay blame?

Headline News (no date supplied)

Agony of parent's discovery

'My son fell prey to the drug scene'

Letter of the week

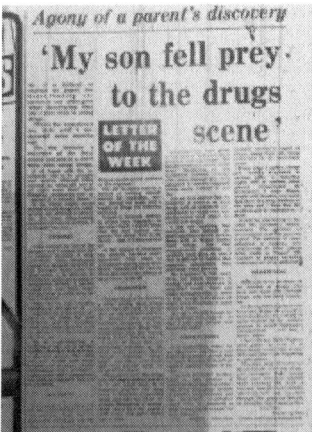

Sir – it is difficult to explain on paper the heart rending experience one undergoes when discovering that one's own child is using drugs. This is the experience m6 wife and I underwent some months ago. My son became a follower of the Soul music cult and in a short time was using drugs. It all began with the occasional visit to an all-night Soul session, although other excuses for being out late or all night were used. Such things as 'missed the bus,' or 'stayed at a friend's house.' In the initial stages, small doses of mild drugs are used as they are difficult to detect. By the time drug taking becomes obvious to parent it's usually too late. **VANISHES** I had warned my son of the dangers and I trusted him not to become involved in drug activities. Once teenagers tasted the dubious delights of the all-night scene and the drug scene it is difficult to keep them away as in today's permissive society a parent has little legal control over a child once he has turned 17. What hit was he virtually vanishes at the age of 18. And once he is on drugs the lure is too great for any deterrent and he becomes more and more devious with his excuses and attempts to cover up. As if experiencing a nightmare, one sees a strong healthy child become a physical wreck. The child one has raised and loved becomes a stranger surly, uncommunicative, deceptive, antagonistic and a compulsive liar with no apparent interest in anything. *APPARENT - Missing text –* fatigue caused by the excesses of the weekend. His job becomes merely a means of raising enough money for cigarettes, beer etc., during the week and a supply of drugs the following weekend. Indeed, it becomes difficult to attend work regularly; on the other hand, I hardly think that the evil swine's who peddle the drugs find it difficult that is if they work at all. As the dosage is increased the affects become more apparent. This leads to youngsters staying away from home sometimes for two or three days until the effects of drugs have worn off. **GRADUATED** The sad thing is that there is a belief among these young users that the type of drugs they use are harmless and can be 'kicked' when required. Another weakness is that many youngsters think they know what they are buying when in fact they do not. I know of drugs that are commonly available at all night music venues. These include 'relaxing,' drugs which are often overdosed and lead to the need for hospital treatment. Drug prices vary the going rate for amphetamine powder is £1 per small dose. It is common practice for drug users to buy lots of assorted drugs and take the lot at intervals throughout a session. Amphetamines were given in this manner to thousands of people in post war Japan. The dangers were not known at the time. Hundreds of the recipients suffered irreversible brain damage and were admitted to mental hospitals were many remain to this day. It is my firm opinion that the majority of addicts on hard drugs such as morphine etc. graduated to them via amphetamine and other so called soft drugs. I'm not implying that everyone who attends all night dance sessions such as those held at Wigan Casino uses drugs. Nor that managements perpetrate or condone what goes on. But I find it difficult to believe that someone somewhere does not know what goes on. My argument is that apart from the lesser dangers of fatigue and over exposure to amplified music there are many teenagers who in order to stay awake and dance all night need stimulants in some form or other. My sons alleged reason for taking drugs was indeed 'so i can stay awake and dance all night.' **PROSECUTIONS** Its fashionable sociologists to say that a bad home background drives kids to drugs. Wanting to dance all night is another reason in my view. I'm sure the police do their best in the matter of prosecutions regarding drugs. The force throughout Britain is gravely undermanned and the necessary conditions which must be observed in (*missing dialogue*) recently carried a report of police doing their job being criticised in no uncertain terms. From what I gather drugs are readily available in various pubs on Saturday nights and in various other places frequented by teenagers. I hope Wigan people become convinced that there is a drug problem in the town and I hope the problem will be stamped on hard. It will be interesting to see what the coroner's enquiry reveals. The number of prosecutions over the past two years? The number of cases admitted to hospital both locally and in other places after visiting Wigan. The number of people receiving treatment for drug addiction. **HEARTENING** What will never be known is the number of people who have lost their jobs through drugs. And lost their friends too. Or the number of people who have left Wigan in the search for hard drugs and the number of cases hushed up by parents anxious to avoid unpleasant consequences 'not that I blame them.' I have always found Wigan a good place to live. It is heartening to see that at last MP's and others are beginning to take notice. This may help stamp out the evil trade involving drugs. Save teenagers from ruining their lives and save parents from reaching the state of nervous and physical debility which my wife and I reached through the gnawing anxiety as Saturday night approaches. (loss of transcription)

Author; As a parent, it is easy to identify with this personal rendition of the travesty that has befallen this family. We recognise that the dangers of drugs are only too apparent now as they were back then. In some respect, today's parents are probably far more aware of the use and the peer pressure that exists in today's more liberal society. It would seem that designer drugs and hard drugs are far more accessible than they were decades ago. Even though the trail of misery that often accompanies cocaine and heroin is well reported, it still attracts new and willing users in prolific numbers daily. Television and films can also portray drug use as cool and almost normal and only when the likes of high profile entertainers like River Phoenix or Amy Winehouse lose their lives to drugs or alcohol, that young people can often take stock. Like an invincible force, young people become caught up in the moment and the desire to have a good time. Recreational drugs will never cease to exist. The government makes money from nicotine and this powerful addictive drug is apparently more addictive than heroine gram for gram. Parliament readily accepts the benefits of the high tax gained from the purchase of cigarettes. The NHS probably survives on the funding and contribution from smokers. Our MP's will except that the diminishing services provided by hospitals are clogged up with the illnesses created from smoking. Congested like the lungs of the people it serves, the health service is allowed to die slowly from a lack of funding. Sold on every street corner, twenty fags can be smoked in plain sight. In front of children, in crowds of shoppers or at the entrance of your local pub. Yes, we have become less tolerant to smokers and it's becoming less acceptable in public places. The seventies had pubs filled with smoke, cinemas and busses were choking its passengers to death by passive smoking. Even flights allowed smoking and I even remember as youngster sitting with the doctor who was happily smoking a Woodbine. If we are now recognising the related diseases caused by the addiction to smoking then why is it still acceptable to sell cigarettes to a sixteen-year-old? I recently visited Amsterdam where drugs were smoked openly in the bars throughout the city. Cigarettes had to be smoked outside in the doorways and the shops were full of space cakes, bong pipes and every other type of drug paraphernalia. Surveys conducted by 'Recovery Brands,' and published by the Mail on line newspaper, showed that Amsterdam didn't even get in the top five countries for cannabis use. Surprisingly Iceland, America and Spain, were shown to smoke more weed than the country that actually legalises its use. The UK was not part of the survey but it seems that the more liberal you are to the substances that can be abused, regardless of constriction, the less relevance they have. That was a long sentence, but not as long as the sentence for drug pushing, or the death sentence for lung cancer. June Brown alias Dot Cotton, has made a living by having a fag drooping from her east end wrinkled mush and none of those thirty million record viewing figures were offended enough to complain. The fact remains, that the law deals with alcohol and drug misuse by following a certain set of guidelines that ensure that no one steps on to their manor. As the profiteers from misery the government will use smoke and mirrors to deflect from the article written above. Drinking and driving kills innocent people year after year and yet you are actually allowed to drink alcohol and drive. Two pints is the recommended guide line from most web sites including the NHS site. This is before explaining units and body weight, and metabolism which can make a difference. Seems to be an invitation to test many people's resolve instead of just having zero tolerance. There are further newspaper stories to follow that will highlight the drug misuse and those differences between a reckless youth and a more disciplined society. The people that attended the Casino were not all reckless and drunk on the cup of youth, they were responsible too. University students, apprentices, builders, business owners and of course unemployed. If you could bring these people back together, there would probably be enough skills to rebuild the old place. That said, during the Casino's heyday, the numbers of unemployed were growing to excessive proportions. Figures show that in 1971 four percent of the UK population were unemployed, by 1981 it had grown to a staggering twelve percent, who found themselves without work. It was not long after 1981 that I found that unemployment hits hard in so many ways. With a family of three young children to care for and the gas cut off, reality soon bites. I knew that I had to sell my treasured collection of four hundred pieces of vinyl. Needs must as they say and this was the days of Alan Bleasdales 'Boys from the Black Stuff.' Like the TV series portrayed at the time, me, my brother and a friend decided to look for work in London. We soon found out that the streets weren't paved with gold and having slept in a van for a week we gave up and came back to face even more misery. By now the Casino had closed down and if I'm honest it was the furthest thing from my mind. A lot of people where I lived were having to work for cash in hand. This was not to fiddle the benefits system as is so often thought, it was purely to survive as is so often overlooked. This may be the United Kingdom but food, heat, rent and school uniforms were not given to one and all. Having no gas or electricity on Christmas Eve is enough to make you feel that the world has abandoned you. No money to buy the shitty card that goes in the shitty metre is bad enough, but having to borrow that money to get that card is almost as bad. And should that card bend as you put it into the slot then it would be nothing more than another slap in the face. Add to this, the wish list of three excited children and you have a some-

119

thing that makes you almost hate Christmas. People like us existed all over the country and I remember so many desperate families scraping along and doing their best to make ends meet. There were jobs on building sites, working knee deep in mud, pushing wheelbarrows full of bricks over sunken planks of wood. There were jobs on farms cutting lettuce that was painfully excruciating and back breaking that lasted only a couple of days. Following tractors along muddy fields soaked by freezing rain, cutting cabbage stems with blunt knives with fingers as cold as ice. You agreed to do everything and anything for any amount of money and you hid in a cupboard if a suited person knocked on the door. My vinyl record collection had been put together with hard earned cash. Sometimes I'd walked eight miles home to add the fare of the bus towards the records I wanted to buy. Those miles and those cherished singles are a distant memory and thirty-five years later I would do the same again willingly. But I'd sell my car first. When I talk to Northern collectors now and mention that I owned a certain record, they ask me what happened to my collection? My real answer should be 'People that's why.'

❖ ❖ ❖

CHAPTER 15

Lend a Hand

As implausible as this may seem, at some point during an all-nighter at Wigan, I would take a well-earned rest and lie on the stage behind one of the large speakers. This area was covered in bags and holdalls of all shapes and sizes. It was here without the aid of narcotics or a hypnotist that I could fall into what could only be described as a semi-conscious state. You may have seen footage of old Indian gurus sleeping on beds of nails, this effectively was the same thing. The stage vibrated constantly and the music still echoed from ceiling to floor with intense purpose, but with a little less volume. Drifting momentarily on a makeshift pillow emblazoned with a sports logo and anniversary badges, the heat of the night cooled just enough to allow some respite. It was while in this horizontal zone that I became unwittingly involved in what I call the 'baggage handlers strike.' Well that's my name for it, robbery is probably the more appropriate description. It all started when one of my swollen size tens was shook in a way as to get my attention but not startle me. I sat up and looked bleary eyed at a familiar face. It was a face that I recognised instantly and had said hello to many times in passing. The person holding my foot was not someone I'd had previous conversation with, just someone who danced regularly near to the stage and close to where I spent most of the night. She had a boyish face and she danced for all intended purposes like a bloke. I'd heard she was gay, or at the time, the title would have been 'Lesbo' or 'Dyke' amongst other synonyms of the seventies. However, this is totally irrelevant with regards to the story except she always struck me as a rogue and I'd heard she also had a drug problem. Worse still I remember all her teeth disappearing over a few months and then in turn she disappeared from the all-nighters. I was told she'd died from a drugs overdose, but I have no inclination to try to dig any further into that aspect to substantiate my story. I remember her name to this day and more so for the event she managed to embroil me into without my knowledge. Miss H as I will call her for the purposes of anonymity, had now gained my attention. She knew my name and with an apologetic smile asked me to hand down the bag she was pointing to. I was surrounded by many bags of all colours, shapes and sizes. She was particular in her choice, thus creating an illusion of ownership. I pointed and she nodded and I passed it down with what I know would have been my happy to help smile. Never the type to speak his mind and say, 'fuck off and leave me alone.' Miss H turned and headed off with the delivered bag up the stairs to the balcony and I returned happily back to my slumber. No sooner had my head melted back into the Adidas bag of uncomfortableness when my foot gets another shake. The same actions are replayed identically to the last awakening except this time the smiling Miss H asks me to pass down a bag which causes some me some concern. 'The red bag,' she says, and points to it with a genuine air of ownership. I look at her and realise that her request is not making sense. 'Pointing at the bag I say, 'that's my bag, what do you mean?' Quick as a pickpocket she apologises and says, 'no I meant the one next to it, it's my mates.' I oblige and believe her mistake was innocent as she melts away into a crowd of people. At some point i must have been disturbed by another bag finder or just the desire to grab a cup of coffee and to leave the stage. Re-joining the remains of the night feeling slightly rejuvenated and ready to grab the last hour or so of Dave Evison's finest. Soon the three before eight would herald the end of another all-nighter and people would start to gather their friends and their belongings. Small groups of people huddled together saying their goodbyes to acquaintances from all over the country. Bags hanging over shoulders, coffee in hand it was time to face the tiresome journey home. With a flick of a switch the lights of the Casino would change the whole atmosphere and the daylight outside was never a welcome sight. I hated the way the lights came on straight after the last spin of 'I'm On My Way.' It was at this very moment that I became unmasked. Spots absolutely thrive on sweaty teenage pores. I'd been cursed with areas of acne since turning thirteen, my back was so bad I couldn't bare it being touched, in fact I wouldn't take my shirt off as I was so embarrassed. My face was less prone to invasion but it still had the power to grow something volcanic overnight. Angry raging spots would greet everybody I met, before I had time to notice their presence and disgustingly squeeze them away onto a mirror. It can steal your confidence having a spotty face so I never hung around for a chat. On this particular morning, I remember gathering around the corner of the stage while we made a collective decision whether to go to the swimming baths or straight to the bus stop and home. While I patiently waited for others to make the decision for me, I wondered if my facial battlefield could tolerate the chlorine yet again. During this contemplation, I became aware of two girls having a conversation that was intensifying by the second. I could hear two broad Lancashire accents questioning each other intently. Their colourful language crossed between them like two tennis players hitting a ball to one another and fast. 'Your fucking kidding, right?' 'I didn't leave it anywhere else why the fuck would I?' 'My purse and five bastard records were in your bag.' 'Sarah the fucking train tickets were in the side zip, I' haven't enough money to buy tickets home have you?' People could hear their predicament and it suddenly dawned on me that I was partly responsible for their misery. I had been press ganged in to the heist and I felt absolutely awful that I was witnessing the results. Miss H was long gone and I felt like a witness at the execution of an innocent man, or should I say women. There was nothing I could do, I'd been involved and I thought that trying to explain this would only dig me in deeper. You begin to think you will end up giving a statement down at the police station and try to defend your participation in the great baggage scam. Somewhere along the interview I'd be fingerprinted and searched. The fear of hurtling off the top diving board and in to the acid bath of Wigan seemed a better option and so I left. It seemed that most of us trusted each other and our bags lay unguarded in all manner of places. Every week I heard of things getting lifted and one of the worse scenarios I ever witnessed was from my own crowd. Again, I have no intention of name dropping and this person is one of those who only frequented the Casino for a few months. This guy was the type of character who had a charming personality but not the type to cross. His large muscular build gave rise to what was perceived as someone who maybe best kept at arm's length. I got on well with this person, but was totally galled by his actions on the bus home one morning. He had stolen what was then a really good ghetto blaster. This portable radio cassette player looked expensive for its time and when he offered it for the buy now price of five pounds it seemed a real steal, or should I say bargain. I, along with everyone else on the bus wanted to own this piece of hi tech equipment and for a fiver it could wash away the guilt of knowing it was stolen. Ridiculous as it may sound no one had five pounds spare as most of us would have spent everything they had, apart from the bus fare home. I clearly remember some of us offering to pay at a later date but all offers were strangely rejected. Mr T as I will call him, suddenly put this marvellous piece of sound equipment on the floor and proceeded to stamp on it violently. It was a painful thing to watch as it disintegrated like a car in a crushing machine at a scrap yard. He then slid open the bus window and launched it towards the pavement without a care for where it landed. In one absurd display of gratification I understood why in the Colosseum they threw the Christians to the lions. Some people don't carry the same values as others. Only Mr T's mother would have told him off for his actions and only she would have had the courage to smack his arse. The rest of us fell silent as he laughed and no one condemned him. A more accurate description of the Casino would begin to look like 'a den of thieves and drug takers.' It doesn't end there, because the most absurd recollection I have involves a gun being pointed at my head. I was told this by someone who was very much like the aforementioned Mr T, who also visited the Casino for only a short period of time. One early morning while strolling around the balcony I got talking to a guy from Liverpool. He sat alone and I remember him being subdued and a little slow in creating sentences. He had dark circles under eyes and thick black shoulder length hair swept back from his forehead. I'd said hello to him in passing as he sat staring coldly along the dimly lit balcony walkway. Trying to recollect his features is not entirely difficult as when he divulged his dark secret to me, I stared in disbelief wondering if what he was telling me was genuine. He had the look of the actor Vincent Schiavelli who played Fredrickson in 'One Flew Over the Cuckoo's Nest.' You may remember the same actor as the ghost in the film 'Ghost,' who shouts, 'get off my train.' My personality makes me either open and friendly or quietly untrusting I try to judge people quickly. Once I've laughed with someone I'm much more comfortable in conversation, until then I'm slightly wary. This person talked to me in a friendly enough way, after all the accent was familiar. It was during our brief conversation that he told me something that has left me wondering for a lifetime if there was any truth in his bizarre confession. He told me that a couple of weeks earlier he had been sitting in the same spot with a gun and pointing it over the balcony. He looked at me with a broad smile on his face, that would not have been out of place on Dr Jekyll. He made the image of a gun with his two fingers then leaned over the balcony and took the position of a sniper. He made the sound of a gunshot and then turned and looked at me again. 'You were dancing,' he said, 'right there below where you always dance.' I gave no reaction I just stared back at him in disbelief. 'Why me?' I asked innocently. 'It was in this bag, 'he said staring down at the hold-all hidden between his feet. I knew from his historical reference that he was not armed on this occasion. That's if he was telling the truth in the first place. 'I wanted to shoot people, can you imagine what it would be like?' He looked at me as if he deserved a reply. I knew at that very moment that this guy was nuts. Whether his story was true or not he sounded totally like Norman Bates long lost brother. He was psychotic no doubt about it and I can't remember how I managed to end our happy conversation but I remember making my way down stairs in total shock. I never noticed him at the Casino again, but I do remember cautiously staring up at the balcony for the next few weeks. This story may seem very far-fetched but I had learned from an early age that the unexpected should always be expected. Aged about six I was pushed into the deep end of Dovecot baths in Liverpool by a boy running past me. I sank quickly to the bottom putting up hardly any resistance. I'm still here because an eagle-eyed person spotted me and hauled me out. I remember watching the bubbles stream in front of my face and I barely struggled. All I need now is someone to try to poison me and I will have more in common with Rasputin than anyone who's ever lived.

CHAPTER 16

Believe It Or Not

Earlier I mentioned the strange fascination with the history and the demise of the people who fleetingly found fame or who otherwise went on to be household names. The same sense of mystery sometimes shrouds the actual group or musicians that created those obscure one-off hits. For decades, the lack of information regarding who the MVP'S were (Turning My Heartbeat Up) caused it to be something of an enigma. The best information we have is that the group known as the 'Combinations,' who later changed their name to 'The Classics,' hailed from Atlanta Georgia. The name MVP'S came from their manager and former baseball player, Don Clendenon who played for the New York Mets. Hitting a record of home runs he earned the title of 'Most Valuable Player, and used those initials to create his groups new name. When it comes to names Sir Thomas John Woodford is not instantly recognisable to most. When you consider the strong icons that an up and coming singer from the U.K may want to style themselves on, Elvis would possibly spring to mind. The swivel-hipped Tom Jones, aka Tom Woodford, apparently based his style on Chuck Jackson and that the classic song 'It's Not Unusual,' was originally written and intended for Sandie Shaw. On a visit to America, Tom Jones met and sang alongside Jackson, performing a duet of 'What I'd say,' at the famous Apollo theatre. Astoundingly, Chuck Jackson was famously hauled off stage during an audition many years earlier.

Being on a stage is a lot safer than being in the audience, or so you would think. One of the cruellest pieces of fate to ever befall an artist performing on stage must belong to the legendary Curtis Mayfield. He became paralysed from the neck down when the rigging fell from a stage set during a charity concert. He was forty-eight years old and from that day on he was to live life as a quadriplegic, never to play the guitar or perform again. Mayfield tragically became a prisoner of his own body and his only crime was to be outstandingly talented. Another prisoner with hidden talents found fame through the bars of music. If ever a producer was searching for a story to base a film score upon, then a quick read of the life story of Johnny Bragg, 'They're Talking About Me,' would surely fit the bill. By the age of sixteen, John Henry Bragg had been convicted of no less than six rape charges and was sentenced to six sentences of 99 years each. At the age of seventeen he was incarcerated into Nashville prison, Tennessee, for crimes which he always denied. Many have said that Bragg was wrongly convicted and under the leadership of reforming governor Frank G Clement he managed to acquire an early release in 1959. Bragg, had entered the world blind from birth and no doubt suffered from receiving little or no education. The best break he ever received was regaining his sight at the age of seven. Ten years later he was behind bars and it was here that he formed the group who were to be known as the 'Prisonaires.' He created the lyrics for the groups songs but the attributes were shared as he could neither read nor write. They became quite famous in and out of the prison as word began to spread regarding their vocal talents. They managed to win themselves a recording contract with Sam Phillips's famous 'Sun Records,' were they made a friend in Elvis Presley who went out of his way to visit them in prison. They also managed to be allowed time to perform concerts outside of prison making appearances at local radio stations on various occasions. Sadly, Bragg found himself returning to prison for violation of his parole and this continued to be repeated, until eventually spending his last day in prison in 1977. On September 2^{nd,} 2004 Johnny Bragg died of cancer. There has been a project created by director Cass Paley who is attempting to bring the story of the Prisonaires to film. There is also a web site which can be found at theprisonaires.com that has some excellent pictures and biographies featuring Johnny Bragg and the other group members. Escaping prison, it seems comes in many different forms be it through music, tunnelling or plane old fashioned killing in self-defence. Mention the name Darrell Banks to any follower of Northern Soul music and it should be as easy, to bring a trio of records to mind. 'Open the Door to your Heart, Somebody Somewhere Needs You,' and of course the lightning fast, 'Angel Baby.' Three glorious heart thumping songs that would make most people's top one hundred. Yet behind these legendary 'never overplayed,' combination of hits lies another story of a life lost in turmoil. Banks was credited with writing 'Open the Door to Your Heart,' for which he gained one hundred percent of the royalties. However, it came to light that it was a shared effort and that 'Donnie Elbert had been the co-writer. A slightly unscrupulous act that took Elbert sometime to prove and prize away from Banks in an effort to be recognised for fifty percent of the royalties. Known as possessing a moody and brooding personality, Banks was labelled as being somewhat unfriendly. There was no mistaking his outstanding vocals, apart from occasionally being compared closely to JJ Barnes. Banks was to lose his life in an incident that has some loose evidence with regards to its reporting. In February 1970, Banks was shot dead by Aaron Bullock an off-duty policeman in Detroit. The circumstances of his death revolved around the fact that Bank's girlfriend was having an affair with Aaron Bullock, who allegedly intervened during a confrontation between Banks and his then girlfriend Marjorie Bozeman. Bozeman was in the process of bringing about a separation from Banks, when Banks apparently pulled a gun on her and Bullock. Bullock reacted quickly and drew his own gun on Banks and shot him in the neck. Banks consequently died later in hospital aged only thirty-five. He was buried in an unmarked grave which was eventually given a headstone in 2004. For me, it seems amazing that I always imagined the people behind the music I loved, to be living the highlife somewhere in America. Surely those of us less talented with a more mundane existence were the most likely to go off the rails. The truth is we do not own tragedy we actually invite it through our own actions. The temptation of drugs and alcohol is shared equally between the rich, the famous and the working class. If ever there was one line of lyrics that portrays empathy regarding tragedy, then it has to be from the wonderful collaboration of Williams and Watson. Larry Williams and Johnny Guitar Watson, managed to put together a couple of minutes of pure therapy in their classic Northern hit 'Too Late.' With the line, *'gone and made you an alcoholic, sorry about that,'* it superbly drips irony into Soul. Larry Williams could almost be accused of writing from experience given the reckless nature of his life. A long-time friend and associate of Little Richard, they both shared a journey into the darkest side of drug abuse and debt. Both addicted to Heroin and living in Los Angeles the two close friends found themselves falling out over a drug debt. Williams was at odds over the fact that Little Richard owed him money for drugs and that he had disappeared from sight. Eventually catching up with Little Richard, Williams stuck a gun in the face of his friend and for some reason thought better of pulling the trigger. Richards found the money to repay the debt and with it found faith in god and became a minister. When asked about these events and turning to god Little Richard mentions how this was indeed the most fearful moment of his life as Larry Williams had become terribly unpredictable through his reliance on drugs. Another strange event which Little Richard claims turned him back to god was when he discovered the plane that he was meant to catch on his return from Sydney Australia had crashed in to the ocean. He noted that the previous evening while performing at an outdoor concert he had spotted a red fireball crossing the sky. He believed that this was a sign from god and a calling. What is it about musicians and planes? Williams was found dead at home in 1980 with a gunshot wound to his head. Declared as suicide the forty-four-year-old Williams death was shrouded in suspicion but nothing proven to the contrary. We owe Williams another debt and that is for the northern Soul classic 'I Don't Want Discuss It.' (You're My Girl). It was during his friendship with Little Richard that he helped produce the album (The Explosive Little Richard) 1966/67. Williams, Watson and Little Richard became a part of the strange world of Northern Soul, partly by chance and partly by design. Jackie Wilson, Marvin Gaye and Sam Cooke are three singers who are the personification of fame. Through their music they have created a following that will survive from generation to generation. But their fame was costly and it wasn't just their outstanding vocals that they had in common. Guns, knives and tragedy came to all these legendary singers like a curse from a horror film. Jackie Wilson who has a plethora of hits that live within the Northern Soul catalogue, was actually shot by a jealous lover. Apparently, a woman by the name of Juanita Jones, shot two bullets in to the stomach of Wilson, which he thankfully survived but it cost him a kidney. This fracas was supposedly due to him having an affair with Sam Cooke's ex-girlfriend. Jackie lived an eventful life idolised by many including the likes of Elvis and other big stars of the time. He was labelled by many as the black Elvis. This did not bring him the same luxuries as Presley and he was intimidated by those around him who controlled the music business. Rumour has it that he was hung upside down by his ankles from a high rise building in order to get him to sign a contract. Other threats included being gagged and bound and locked in a rat-infested cellar to ensure that he abided by the demands from those executives who viewed him as property. Believed to have been owed over one million dollars in royalties the singer was never in a position to contest his claim through the courts. Jackie collapsed on stage when performing in New Jersey while singing 'Lonely Teardrops.' A heart attack which resulted in a coma basically ended Jackie's life as he knew it. Destined to spend the next nine years in a nursing home in a vegetative state it was not a fitting end to such a great artist. He died penniless on the 21st of January 1984. He appeared at the Casino on the 14th June 1975 where many of those who were lucky enough to have attended that night have said he wasn't at his expected best. Rumour has it that he was already showing signs of ill health and this was to be his last performance in the U.K. He sadly collapsed at a venue in New Jersey called the Latin Casino. His long-term friend Sam Cooke was not as lucky as Jackie when it came to escaping death via gun shots. His life was ended by a bizarre turn of events which took place at a motel in Los Angeles California. It was December 1964 when the thirty-three-year-old Cooke was found dead at the Hacienda motel, bizarrely half naked, in what seemed to be an act of retribution. Shot dead by Bertha Franklin in the manager's office of the motel, Cooke became the subject of a myriad of conspiracy theories. Elisa Boyer had struck up conversation with Cooke at a night club and returned to the motel where the evening took a strange turn of events. she believed that she was about to be raped. While Cooke was in the bathroom, Boyer took the opportunity to escape from the room, taking some of Cooke's clothing as she did so. Cooke gave chase and it was alleged that he grappled with Franklin demanding to know where Boyer had gone. Claiming that both she and Cooke ended up wrestling to the floor, Franklin managed to get up and locate a gun that was kept in the office. She shot Cooke in self-defence and the jury classed this as justifiable homicide. There are reports that just over a hundred dollars in cash was found in the room that Cooke had hired. It is also believed that Cooke was seen to be carrying far more cash than what was recovered, earlier in the evening by eye witnesses. Boyer was arrested a year later for prostitution and from the Coroner and other authorities, we were informed that Cooke's last words were, 'lady you shot me.' A sad end to a legendary singer. But legends are created when they leave us wanting more. They seem to leave us in the untimeliest fashion. Buddy Holly, Otis Reading, Patsy Cline, John Denver, Lynyrd Skynyrd, Ricky Nelson, Jim Reeves, all of whom died in plane crashes. A couple of years ago I was on a night flight to Los Angeles with Bruno Mars, if I'd have known then what I know now I'd have got the next flight. Fortunately, my wife and I didn't recognise him, sorry Bruno. He kept coming to ask his entourage if they were 'ok' back there in economy class, while he no doubt quaffed champagne further forward in business class. Being a night flight the plane was very dimly lit apart from the odd reading light. I couldn't understand why all these Schwarzenegger clones where all wearing sunglasses? Bruno was also wearing sunglasses, so he probably couldn't see them and they couldn't see him. When we finally exited LA airport the next morning we saw the Mars Crewe pushing big black trunks on wheels with the name Bruno Mars emblazoned all over them. My wife looked up his name on Google and triumphantly turned to me and said, 'he's a pop star and he's playing here tonight.' *That's what I like,'* it just cost us more in data usage looking him up than it was to buy a ticket to see him in concert. Bruno also sings about catching grenades for people, as well as catching flights, so legendary status is only a matter of time.

◆ ◆ ◆

HELP ME

Headline News

Plea from the Soul

'Give back my discs or I'm finished'

Plea from the soul

Give back my discs or I'm finished

Butcher's tale of heartache

The theft of 400 rare and valuable records could force a top Wigan DJ to give up his career. For Russ Winstanley has spent years building up the collection of Soul records that were stolen from Wigan Casino last Sunday night. Russ who is one of the country's leading Soul DJ's said this week: 'if I don't get these records back I will have to consider giving up DJ work. Most of the records were worth at least £5 and there are only one or two copies of some of them available. **SEARCH** When the theft was discovered the people in the Casino were searched but nothing was found. Russ added 'it looks like ******* missing text ****** belonging to other DJ's in the room but they only took mine. The records that were in a brown teak finish box included 'Milton Wrights' 'I belong to you and Danny Williams's (of Moon River fame) Who's Little Girl, Are You?' Russ has offered a £50 reward to anyone who can give information leading to the recovery of the records. If anyone has any information they can contact Russ at Wigan ****** Only 12 months ago a number of records were stolen from Rush's shop in Hallgate, Wigan. But here were later returned.

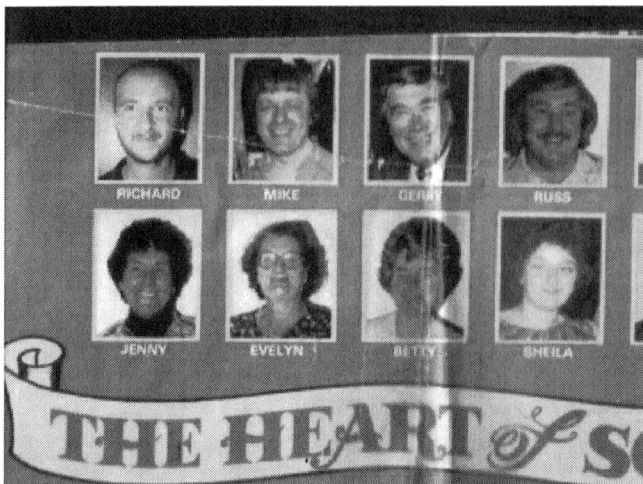

Author: I would imagine that Russ was gutted to say the least. Reading between the lines it was like 'why me?' there were other boxes in the room to choose from. Ah but did they have a teak finish? Using the tradition of the board game of Cluedo we should ask. Was it Betty in the ballroom with the spanner? Or perhaps it was Evelyn in the kitchen with candlestick or Gerry in the cellar with the lead pipe.

Headline News

A phone call and DJ Russ is in a spin again.

Wigan Observer: May 13, 1973

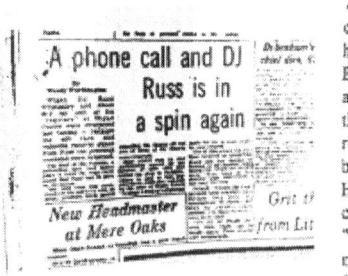

A phone call and DJ Russ is in a spin again.

By Wendy Worthington

Wigan DJ Russ Winstanley and about 99.9 percent of the regulars at Wigan Casino were overjoyed last Sunday- because the 400 rare and valuable records stolen from Russ the previous weekend were returned. The theft of the records, a collection that had taken years to build up, may have meant that Russ had to give up his career. But, said Russ this week, thanks to the publicity and no doubt, pressure attending the Casino all but two or three of the records were returned. Russ added he was particularly moved by the number of kids who had visited his shop at Hallgate willing to give to him any records he could use and also by the offer of Wigan Casino to stage a kind of testimonial night to raise money for new records. One of this area's top DJ's, Russ received an anonymous phone call last Sunday afternoon at his parents' home telling him were the records were. They were in 5 plastic bags underneath a car near his shop. He said it looks like it was someone local who stole them because they knew my whereabouts on Sunday and even my parents phone number. I'm really relieved to have them back. It's not as if they were tools which can be bought back again. These records were irreplaceable.

Author: What a nice happy ending and an open and shut case. It must have been the brown teak box they were after, as the records were dumped in plastic bags. I recall seeing a yellow Ford Cortina with a teak dashboard parked outside the Council offices around this time. All but two of the records were returned. The ones reported missing were, Eddie Parker, 'I'm Gone,' Madeleine Bell, 'Picture Me Gone.' Or maybe not? The report says, 'kids were willing to give Russ any records he could use.' I can almost imagine the avalanche of 'Skiing in the Snow' and the dozens of 'Footsee' records being dropped off at his shop. All generously donated by Wigan's Ovation, Wigan's Chosen Few and Wigan's 'I purchased crap society.' I wanted more than this. I was admittedly disappointed by this article, thinking it could have been so much more. I wanted ransom notes made out of newspaper cuttings and sliced up pieces of vinyl posted through the letter box. I wanted to read about threats demanding money or the vinyl kidnapper would start to get nasty. ' I want one thousand pounds left in a suitcase in a deserted phone box on the outskirts of Wigan at midnight or I start to take out the hostages one by one. 'Gerri Granger, **will** go to pieces.' The conversation would be totally Northern Soul.

Vinylnapper - '*Better use your head* , **Russ, if you want to see Lorraine Silver again.'**

Russ - '*That's my girl,*' if you so much as scratch her I'll kill you.'

Vinylnapper - '*You gotta pay the price,*' if you want to get these people released Russ.

Russ - '*You got me were you want me, what can I do.*'

Vinylnapper - '*Cashing in,* **Russ** '*you gotta pay your dues.*'

Russ - '*Name it you've got it,* just don't hurt them.' *'I'll pay the price.*'

Vinylnapper - '*6* '*o'clock, I'll call you on the Hot line.*'

Bordering on a thriller straight out of Hollywood the five plastic bags would have contained the remnants of the Ron Grainer Orchestra. 'So, this would-be thief runs off with a heavy teak box full of records. Are we looking for a man with a hernia?' He rings the parents of the person who he stole from, did he find them in the Wigan and greater Manchester phone book? Did he ring forty-seven Winstanley's in that phone book before getting the right people? Did he say 'is that Russ's mum, I've got your sons collection here? I feel reet guilty tha knows so I'm gonna put them under a Ford Capri in some Co Op bags where he can find them. I made a terrible mistake and I realised how bad it was when I played one called the Wigan Joker by the all-night band.' It was a great outcome that Russ managed to get his records returned. (According to the journalist, we were 'over-joyed) Getting one record stolen is bad enough but getting your whole collection is soul destroying. Talking of soul destroying, records like, The Wigan Joker, Six by Six and Joe 90 were in my opinion utter shite, however I am sure that other people may find them musically entertaining. They are of course entitled to make their own judgement as to what is and what isn't good Northern Soul. There, I've said it, I'm being non-judgmental. I'm respecting other people's decisions. Just because they're tone deaf with the same IQ as a jelly fish, it still means they sure know how to 'keep the faith.' By the way, before I stir up a hornet's nest, if you want to tell me to 'keep the faith, or put KTF at the end of internet comments, you go ahead and do so, it's a free country, so they tell us. Wtf.

By 1981 the Casino was not the powerhouse it had been. Foot-fall was down and as numbers dwindled the prospect of the doors closing for good seemed only a matter of time. The following press release celebrated the Casinos anniversary, focusing on the 500th all-nighter. There seems to be a mixed review which leans closely to eulogising the Casino and its history while fighting its cause.

HEADLINE NEWS

Wigan Observer Thursday May 14[th,] 1981

The Hot 500th and they said it wouldn't last!

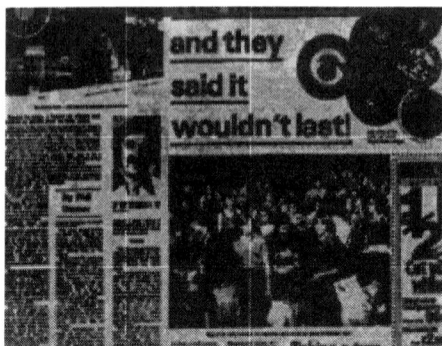

Seamy to some, a haven to others and doomed to failure after its first night. Just a few of the many opinions expressed of Wigan's famous Casino All-nighters. Now this one night wonder is to celebrate its 500th anniversary on Saturday, and despite the recession, the disco boom and the resurgence of heavy metal, it is still going as strong as when it began. It was at 2.00 on a Saturday morning, September 23 back in 1973 that Gerry Marshal the late Mike Walker and DJ Russ Winstanley started what was to be a phenomenal success and so brought the attention of the country to the sound known as Northern Soul. Although Northern Soul was already popular at places such as the Torch in Stoke and had its foundations at venues at the Wheel in Manchester, it was the Wigan Casino that captured the imagination of the country and thrust the music into the limelight. Suddenly the whole of Britain was made aware of music that did not depend upon the ephemeral gloss of glitter. All you needed was some loose clothing and the stamina to dance away for up to eight hours throughout the night. Wiganers didn't know what had hit them *(author: we soulies knew what it was like when a Wiganer hit us)* youngsters travelled from literally all over the country to converge on what was the old Empress ball room and danced until dawn and beyond to records most of which had never within a thousand places of the top ten. Often over a thousand-people queued outside the Casino on a Saturday night, armed with a variety of bags and holdalls for a change of clothes. Many had spent the equivalent of a week's wages just to reach their shrine.

After the dancing, back flops, spins and eight hours of non-stop stomping to sounds unfamiliar outside those four sweat laden walls, they would finally drag their weary way home or spend a Sunday morning quietly snoozing in the spectator's area of Wigan baths.

APPLICATIONS Now this weekly event is to have its 500th birthday and the endless procession of tired All-nighters still continues. One of its longest serving stalwarts has been top DJ Russ Winstanley, who's idea of a soul All-Nighter was at first greeted with cynicism....until 2.00am that Saturday morning. 'I used to DJ at Newtown British Legion,' he said, 'and I kept getting asked more and more for Northern Soul. I'd heard that the Torch in Stoke was finishing and had just started working on Wigan market selling Soul imports and the like. So as a joke I suggested starting an All-Nighter at the Wigan Casino. Gerry Marshal was the manager at the time and he finally agreed to put one on. On the first night, we got 650 people at one pound each. We also received thousands of applications for membership to join when we put an advertisement in the Blues and Soul magazine. It just took off and we went from strength to strength.' The peak of the Casino for Russ was 1974 to 1976 the year when Wigan's Chosen Few hit Top of The Pops and Wigan's Ovation we're riding high in the charts. Then came the punk era and recession. (Author: sorry couldn't help but break in here, but did Russ really say this was the peak of the Casino for him? Well coming from the man who started the dam thing rolling and brought the likes of Edwin Star and Jackie Wilson to the stage, to name but a few, I'm damned if I believe that was his peak. Oh, and I don't believe the punks were responsible for the recession either.) For most of the country the music had to reflect the gloom of the dole queues and Northern Soul became last year's fashion. However, the All-Nighters would not die, although for a time it looked as if the Casino would be pulled down. But despite the threats from so many quarters the All-Nighters continued and perhaps really showed for the first time why they were and still are so popular. 'The All-Nighters did drop off with the recession,' said Russ, but not too much because they offered something you could not get at one or two places in the country. Obviously, the music was number one' but people also came, and still do, I think because of the tremendous atmosphere. There's a great feeling of friendliness and a sense of belonging you don't really find in other clubs. **CARDS** 'We always get birthday cards from people and congratulations sent to us on our anniversary's, how many other discos can claim that? It shows you the kind of support we get where over 800 people regularly turn up. They come from all over the country from Southampton to Dundee and just think how much it costs them. Lots of them will work hard all week and then come here and enjoy themselves. That's the kind of people we get and that's the attraction of the Casino.' The past 500 All-Nighters have seen many acts like Edwin Starr and Tommy Hunt, and can proudly boast of helping to launch quite a few records into the British charts. Frankie Vallis 'The Night, 'Detroit Spinners, 'Working My Way Back to You,' and The Miracles 'Love Machine, 'to name but three, as well as several records on its own Casino Classics label. The Casino has also had a hand to play in the British success of Tavares and the late composer Ron Grainer, who had a close connection with the place. It's DJs have become national figures in the discos and it can proudly boast that it possesses the words rarest record, Frank Wilson's 'Do I Love You' of which only one promotional copy survives and which is valued at more than £1,000 (only superseded by Bob Dylan's 'Superstate 80' bootleg) And so the Casino must look to the future. A film is to be made along the lines of 'Quadrophenia' and a couple of books chronicling the All-Nighter's colourful history have been prepared. **CUTTING** But at the same time heavy metal and 'Futurist' music is making fresh inroads and the recession is cutting deeper into people's pockets and their livelihoods. However, the Casino All-Nighters will survive the storm simply because of the music. As Russ stated, 'Northern Soul' could be seen as thinking person's alternative. It will always be there. Even at the height of Saturday Night Fever and the Funk and Disco boom there was always an underground scene. People may say were trapped in a time warp but we keep coming back. **EXPLODE** 'Heavy metal music will explode on the scene again over the next few years and it will be just like the early 70s all over again. Northern Soul will do the same. 'There will always be a Northern scene and I definitely hope to be a part of it for as long as I can.' Sentiments echoed no doubt by the massive ranks of All-Nighters. Fashions may change and times may be hard but for those who continue to 'keep the faith' the beat will go on forever and despite the odds they'll hope to carry on stomping and enjoying themselves for at least another 500 All-Nighters.

Author: If we can believe all that was written in this interview and take it on face value, I would hazard a guess that Russ could see the writing on the wall. For sure he is the only person who could substantiate that claim but it does read as a retirement speech. 'Thank you all for coming.' However, I give Russ his due in the fact that he also made statements in which he was proven categorically correct. He mentions, 'there will always be a Northern Soul scene,' somewhat brave given a year later the doors finally slammed shut on the Casino for good. He also pays homage to the people who travelled long distance to get to the Casino and about the cost involved during a recession. Although he would have done well to remember that when it came to the last all-nighter that never was. He also mentioned the legends that graced the Casino such as Edwin Starr and Tommy Hunt. Given the opportunity to rethink this interview from today's perspective I'll bet that Russ would see the peak of his Casino, from an entirely different view point. I may be wrong but Russ will always be affectionately known as 'Russ Winstanley creator of the Casino,' can you really top that accolade?

❖ ❖ ❖

CHAPTER 17

Have Love Will Travel

The problem with having Wigan Casino on your doorstep is you can be forgiven for not wanting to experience another location. We had the best All-Nighter less than thirty minutes bus drive away. On rare occasions, I ventured to pastures new but never found anything that matched the Casino for sheer atmosphere. I went to the Queens Hall in Bradford and the Ritz all-dayers in Manchester, good but not great. I've been to many other venues since the Casino closed and sadly they all paled in comparison. I'd come to the conclusion very early in my travelling days, it was no wonder people journeyed hundreds of miles to get to Wigan on a Saturday night. Amongst those who travelled a good distance were the Darlington crowd. Avid followers of the scene and always well represented, these tough people of the north east made many friends. It's strange how the Skelmersdale crowd seemed to latch on to anyone with an accent that had a hint of Geordie twang. Before I ignite a ton of dynamite, I do acknowledge that there is a lot of pride when it comes to belonging to a certain location. Woe be tide addressing anyone from Middlesbrough as being from Newcastle and vice a versa. Me and my mate had started to see a couple of girls from Darlington and they happened to be sisters. Relationships at the Casino were hardly a serious commitment. Basically, it was a romantic ordeal that was doomed to failure, just like 'Romeo and Juliet,' or like 'Adam and Eve.' My younger brother used to sum it up by saying 'you can't get your nuts through the post.' He was right and he possessed the driest sense of humour I have ever known to this day. He took the piss out of anything remotely connected to Northern Soul and it was like being roasted by Jack Dee every week. He had good taste in music and never found anything that I played worth listening to. He'd bounce around the house singing 'Nine Times Out of Ten,' doing his version of an exaggerated soul dance. He was quick to point out the error of my ways when I purchased 'It's Raining Men,' and I took sweet revenge when he thought Boy George was a girl and bought Culture Clubs first album 'Kissing to Be Clever.' A bit of karma to the comedian. I'm not homophobic in the least but strange choices that we can't deny, along with the fact my sister used to dress me as a brownie at the age of four. As if trying to prove an old adage that 'absence indeed makes the heart grow fonder,' my friend and I set off for Darlington one weekend. Our long-distance girlfriends had not been able to get down to Wigan for a couple of weeks, so we decided to pay them a visit, at their own local All-Nighter. Rosey Jones, 'Have Love Will Travel,' and we intended to live up to it like a couple of love sick puppies. The train journey was bloody awful and if it wasn't for our high levels of testosterone, we'd have probably got off half way there and turned sensibly back. We arrived at Darlington train station with only the name of Newton Aycliffe and some meeting room or hall as our final destination. We soon realised that saying you're from Darlington and actually living in Newton Aycliffe is the equivalent of saying you live in the Isle of Man just off Lancashire. Our feet where about to be introduced to the harshest geography lesson that would last a life time. We opted to use our limited reserves of cash to get a taxi to Newton Aycliffe just outside Darlington. So, two lads with very broad Scouse accents jump into a taxi and say something similar to, 'alright mate, take us to da all-nighter in d' Newton Aycliffe.' The thoughtful taxi driver was kind enough to take us around the sites of Darlington first, showing us that this was the only place in the U.K. with two town halls and two Woolworths. Our journey into expense landed us outside a large sports complex. Fleeced but with hearts pumping we recognised the music pouring out of the venue like a guard of honour welcoming royalty. My young fervent imagination had visions of two young surprised girls running in slow motion into both mine and my friend's arms. Heroes who had made a special quest being faithfully adored for our efforts. It didn't go exactly to plan in-fact it was quite the opposite. It was like we had walked in wearing eu' de skunk. Our damsels were distressed, so much so they declined to let their hair down and buggered off within minutes of our arrival. All that was needed at this point in the evening was for the DJ to have played Eddie Holman, 'Where I'm Not Wanted.' Although disappointed we decided to make the most of it and actually went on to have a really good night. We danced like the world was watching, we were pretty good movers my friend and I, so we entertained. Like two missionaries from deepest darkest Wigan, we showed those who'd never been to the Casino what it was all about. By the end of the night and into the early morning we began to contemplate the journey home. We'd made some new friends along the way, but we were now alone and staring into the bleak morning light. The winter sun wasn't the only thing that had dawned upon us. No girlfriends, no money and a hundred and twenty-six miles to get home. With our love lives in tatters and our pockets lighter than expected we decided to walk back to Darlington. After a few miles, we realised why the taxi had been so expensive the previous evening, the landscape that surrounded the main road was baron. Surrounded by nothing but countryside, and the odd inquisitive look from a few uncaring cows. Not the first time in the last few hours I might add. A good few weary miles away from the All-Nighter based in the twilight zone, the hunger pangs suddenly began to stab mercilessly. We'd survived on the food of love so far, which turned out to be cold and frozen. Fortunately, I always carried emergency rations and this came in the shape of a tin of apricots. I always put something in my bag just in case I'd spent up on records and it was not unknown for me to be having some weetabix and milk borrowed off a doorstep and consumed in a phone box. Yes, I really did have a bowl and spoon in my bag. My mate Steve went on to join the army, I guess I introduced him to basic survival training. The sight of the Wigan train pulling in to Darlington was far more welcoming than the sisters of sanctimony. Jumping into a warm carriage having shared a small waiting room with a tramp was heaven sent. The scent of the tramp however was far from heavenly. Somewhere beneath a pile of newspapers and cardboard lay a human being that had the ability to snore and hum at the same time. I don't know who I felt sorry for most, this homeless gentleman or us. The choice was simple, either share this two bench miniature waiting room and stay slightly warm or stand outside in the freezing cold. I do get upset by the plight of the homeless and believe that came close to splitting the apricots three ways had we not have devoured them earlier. Sitting comfortably on our homeward bound train and now miles away from the coldest waiting room outside of the arctic circle we both began to doze off. Anyone who has been to an All-Nighter and who is not full of drugs will tell you that the sleep that follows is as deep as it gets. Combined with the warmth of a shared cup of tea and the gentle rocking of the carriage, it's as if you have fell into a giant marshmallow without a care in the world. We could rest easy until arriving in Lancaster where we were to change trains for Wigan. We both woke simultaneously startled by an unfamiliar noise. We had arrived in Lancaster but there was no sight of a platform or any other passengers. Startled by our presence a woman with a vacuum cleaner made haste to turn it off and confront us. It turned out that we had been in to Lancaster station but the train had then reversed back out of the station having now terminated its journey. It had moved to a siding away from the station and was now out of operation. We explained were we had been to this understanding cleaner who showed us a simple safe route back to the main platform. We finally managed to get on to a Wigan train and continue our journey home. Over the next couple of weeks, we told all those who'd listen how good the All-Nighter had been and that it was worth going again. We hired a mini bus and ten of us ventured off to the outskirts of Darlington once more. My friend Steve Rivers who didn't think our last adventure up north was punishing enough roped his father into driving the van. That caveat came with the pleasure of him sleeping in the van overnight. This massively kind gesture from Steve's dad came with one slight concern, he hadn't driven for well over ten years. This became increasingly obvious as Steve argued with his dad telling him that the hard shoulder was not a motorway lane. As we travelled merrily along that hard shoulder for many miles it seemed that the twilight zone was beckoning once more. Thankfully we avoided the ten o'clock news and arrived without incident ,all in one piece and a good night was had by all. In the morning, we headed back towards the motorway tired and hungry. Steve's dad who had now rekindled his driving skills was now driving like Stirling Moss rather than someone gathering moss. We made the decision to stop at the nearest service station for a hot drink and a bit of breakfast. Before arriving at our welcome break I'd noticed that a friend of mine had fallen into a deep sleep. He was sat next to me, mouth open and probably in his mind at home in bed or nestled deeply into that marshmallow. Before we parked up I had loaned a lipstick from one of the girls and took the liberty of dotting his face with anything up to a hundred bright red spots. This was a bad misjudgment on my behalf when I later found out he was a black belt in martial arts. He was actually an instructor, if I'd have known this at the time I certainly wouldn't have even considered it. I begged everyone to keep a straight face and they duly obliged. In the service station my friend remarked how he was getting some strange looks and felt uneasy. We returned to the van and somehow my thoughtless prank was never discovered. For which I'm eternally grateful as in later days I was hunted down and asked why I'd done it. I did the right thing and owned up to it being another person in the van. This forever gave me protection as the guy in question blamed me in return.

Thus, causing a conundrum for who should get a pasting off the karate kid. Narrowly avoiding a scene from 'Enter the Dragon,' we continued on our journey. Soon we began to feel that we were heading in the wrong direction. Somehow Steve's dad had found his way back on to the north bound carriageway. When we realised we were going back to where we'd come from we slipped off the motorway. We ended up at a toll bridge that you had to pay fifty pence to get over. Whilst paying we asked for directions to Liverpool, whereupon we were told to do a u turn and cross back over the bridge and take a certain road. The toll booth attendant made us pay to cross again. Sometime after returning home I think most of us came to the conclusion that travelling wasn't for us, home is where the heart is. And the heart of Northern Soul was Wigan Casino. One can only imagine the mishaps, missed connections and miseries that some people must have endured to get to Wigan from all over the country. I think it is these people who were the 'heart of Soul,' it relates to them more than anyone.

Headline News

Wigan Observer 21.03.1975

Wigan's Ovation set off for hit

Wigan has done it again. Not content with 'Footsee' by Wigan's Chosen Few reaching number four in the hit parade another record has been released again associated with Wigan Casino and the Northern Soul scene, which now stands at number 29 in the top fifty. The record is an old American hit 'Skiing in the Snow' and has been recorded by Wigan's Ovation. The members of the group are Peter and Phillip Preston of Orell Road, Orell, Alfred Brooks and Jim McClusky both of Bolton. After calling in at the Casino 'All-Nighter' last year the lads decided to write a song themselves. The song inspired by the 'All-Nighter' is on the B side of their new record called 'Northern Soul Dancer' it certainly is appropriate to the current Soul scene in Wigan.

HEADLINE NEWS

Wigan Observer December 16, 1977

'Leave us alone' rap for TV. The message to Granada Television came over loud and clear from Wiganers this week: 'Leave our town alone unless you can present a true picture.'

Following yet another programme- 'Wigan Casino,' shown on Monday night – which concentrated yet again on the 'clogs and shawl' image of the town, Wigan people voiced their protests. For although the programme purported to be about the 'going's on' within the Casino's All-Nighter Soul Club it was interspersed with views of Wigan, mainly of what little derelict property there is left. **LOT'S OF CALLS** Twenty-five people who work in the Education Department at Wigan Metro have signed a petition in a bid to get a true picture of Wigan shown. The petition has been sent to Granada along with the comment: Whilst we are proud of Wigan's industrial past we fail to see what relevance it has to present day 'Wigan Casino.' A Metro spokesman said, 'we have had a lot of phone calls complaining about the image of Wigan shown on the programme but it was nothing to do with the council.' Mr Alan Wright researcher for the programme at Granada said that by Tuesday afternoon only two adverse calls had been received by them. Ex Wiganers have also voiced their protests. Mrs X now living Kelso Scotland, wrote to the Wigan Observer: 'I just feel downright ashamed by ITV's biased one-sided view of a wonderful town. How did they find such shots of parts of the town?' Can they not show the good with the bad?' Mr Wright said that members of the All-Nighter had phoned Granada to congratulate them on their capture on film of the atmosphere of the Soul sessions. Viewers were allowed to take a peek at what draws these thousands of young people to Wigan Casino every Saturday for a marathon dance. And the attraction contrary to popular opinion it seems is not drugs, said Mr Wright. 'There may have been a drug problem at the All-Nighter two years ago when a small minority took or peddled soft drugs, but you would get that kind of thing in any nightclub. 'I think the problem at the Casino has been solved partly by a clamp down by the police but also by the members themselves who are so afraid that the Casino might be closed because of drugs that they themselves act as the best possible police force.'

Author: Two short newspaper stories that deliver contrasting viewpoints on the commercial aspects of Wigan. The first story explaining that a local band has used the current appeal of Northern Soul to break into the charts. Initially I was about to tell of my dislike of anything connected with the piggy back tactics of making a fast buck out of the success of Wigan Casino. That was until I came across a web page created by Jim McClusky under the title of Wigan's Ovation. Refreshingly to the point, Jim tells of the groups background and their honest struggle to capture the public's eye. Playing to audiences between the bingo sessions in working men's clubs he was a genuine fan of Northern Soul and visited the Casino when gigging anywhere near home. He tells briefly of how Mike Walker became the groups manager but felt there was little direction or input from his side. Before changing their name to Wigan's Ovation, they were known as Sparkle, which was chosen to reflect the glam rock image of the time. Jim touches on the fact that he and Mike Walker had known each other for many years and actually attended the same school. Jim also revealed that Mike Walker was in a band called Pendulum and was a singer and bass player in his earlier years. He played alongside Alfred Brooke's who later helped form Wigan's Ovation. When Jim and the band were invited to London by Spark records to record their version of Skiing in the Snow,' it must have felt like it was the big break they were looking for. Jim also described how he felt they were ripped off by their promoters but decided that this was not something to elaborate upon on. Jim McClusky writes an honest account of his brief encounter with fame and it is because of this that I can appreciate what that meant to him. As much as I don't particularly like 'Skiing in the Snow,' I also admit there are plenty out there that do. It's a dour remake of the original Invitations hit that was first brought on to scene by Ian Levine. Wigan Ovations remake went some way to stabbing northern soul firmly in the back. By appearing on Top of The Pops in wide trousers and stitched up in Northern Soul badges, it was the worst possible advert for the Casino possible. This toxic misrepresentation gave the outside world the impression of a white soul movement that had as much credence as nun running a brothel. It caused many to feel that the legacy and exclusivity of Northern Soul had been exposed and betrayed. Thrust into the daylight from its once safe underground environment, it had now sent an open invitation to the bandwagon and all those who'd jump on it. We shouldn't blame Jim McClusky and his fellow band members, by all accounts they'd grafted the hard way and were only musicians plying their trade. As per usual there is some that see low hanging fruit and plunder it for all its worth, until it is stripped bare. Jim touched on the sad and surprising suicide of Mike Walker. At that time Mike was the director of RK records, owned then by Richard Kingston, which makes for interesting reading should you look this up via the net. There are links that take the reader to lists of records featuring JJ Barnes and the, All Night Band. All released on Casino Classics. Others include Diane Foster, Ron Grainer and The Wigan Joker and many more who featured on this label. Many Casino members would have seen Mike dashing around the Club at a hundred miles an hour during an all-nighter managing to smile at each and every one of his guests as if he knew them all personally. He was very much a spokesman for the Casino and every so often would take to the stage to make an announcement. On the night, his death was announced I remember a genuine heartfelt sadness from every person who was in the building that night. When the rumours began to spread of how he had died it lacked any other substance, other than he had taken his own life. By this, I mean it was a mystery to those who knew him and a sad loss to those people who viewed him as a driving force behind the Casino's success. Somewhere amongst this conundrum of myths and legends there is the quest for understanding. From the outset, I mentioned being an onlooker with a membership card and a love of the music, nothing more. There was, without doubt another level to the Casino beyond the dance floor. Some coin was to be made by association. Wigan's Ovation and other records like the Footsee created a kind of hybrid of Northern Soul, which didn't sit comfortably into the record boxes of the purists. It was like asking a Shetland pony to race a thoroughbred horse and jump the fences of the Grand National. The punters would see a loser but would be interested for a short time. Like the Emperor's new clothes, eventually some honest person would point out that there's something missing. I bought into the Casino Classics label for 'Shake a Tail Feather' and 'How Long,' with 'Panic.' by Reparata and the Delrons. A good selection and still worth a listen today. But the choice of music associated with the Casino Classics label, falls very short of the mark thereafter and once again I question the sincerity of what was marketed under the banner of 'Classic' Northern Soul. 'A Sting of Brass?'

The second short newspaper article reflects on the image of Wigan portrayed in a TV documentary. I think this may be in response to the documentary entitled 'This England,' which tallies up with the articles date of 1977. The landscapes of many industrial towns in the seventies were similar to Wigan. Cloth caps and coal was an image that was stereotypical of Northern life and many parts of Wales too. It seems that some exception was taken to this bland portrayal and the producers of the film had certainly angered the locals. All 25 of them. Close to an uprising there were rumours that an angry mob wanted to put this film crew into the stocks. Allegedly the Town Crier had summoned the witch finder general to bring them to justice. Meanwhile Mrs X from Kelso Scotland was downright ashamed of the way Wigan had been depicted. Mrs X was obviously proud of her home town, so much so she had put pen to paper. From a 170.3 miles, away to be exact. 'There's no place like home,' she wrote, before clicking her heels and climbing into her own self inflated hot air balloon. Living in Skelmersdale for the best part of twenty years, you eventually learn a thing or two about your close neighbours. Wiganer's where known as 'woolly backs' or 'pie eaters,' both names they found slightly offensive. The first name relates to the days when the farm lads would load the sheep on to the sailing ships leaving Liverpool. The Lancashire farm hands would throw the sheep over their shoulders to walk up the gang plank and deposit the livestock in to a pen. The Scouse sailors would be looking on at this menial task and christened these people 'woolly backs.' The nickname 'Pie Eater,' came from the days of the 1926 miners' strike. Forced through starvation to return to work before other colliery workers they were seen to be eating humble pie. Many people from Wigan will tell you it's due to the fact they are renown for eating a large quantity of pies. Either way, there was no yellow cobbled road leading in or out of Wigan and therefore Mrs X had to accept the truth when it came to the locations chosen. Cobbled streets and tall smoking factory chimneys were all the rage back then and bowler hats were only found in London. Wigan has a long proud history, so before I end up on a wanted poster or living like Salman Rushdie, I'd like to delight Mrs X with the following credits. Once a Celtic town that ruled most of Northern Britain, Wigan succumbed to the Romans. The area was known as Coccium and later in life it became a borough under the instructions of King Henry lll. Eventually becoming a mining town after the first mine was established in 1450. It then went on to have over a 1,000 pit shafts within an area of five miles of the town centre. When it comes to sports, Wigan's Rugby and football teams have played at the highest standard.

◆ ◆ ◆

CHAPTER 18

Ain't That Peculiar

There are many fascinating facts connected to the history of Motown and Northern Soul. Common knowledge to some and yet surprising to others. I never tire of discovering something that has an element of 'bet you didn't expect that.' For instance, it was Ronnie White of the Miracles who discovered Stevie Wonder, after hearing him sing his own song entitled 'lonely boy,' he was aged 11 years old at the time. The Fabulettes were formerly known as the Marvell's who were best known for their record 'Screaming and Shouting, 'their lead singer was Annette Snell. Annette was killed in a plane crash in 1977 after her flight was hit by lightning in Atlanta Georgia. They say that flying is the safest form of transport, however this book is going a long way to dispel that myth. The Ad-libs 'New York in the Dark,' were originally asked to call themselves 'The Cheerio's,' after the breakfast cereal they were asked to promote, they refused. Frankie Vallis real name is Francis Castelluccio. The O'Jays were formerly known as the Mascots. Lynne Randall 'Stranger in My Arms,' was born in Liverpool and emigrated to Australia when she was five. She was a massive celebrity in the sixties and once supported the Monkees and Jimmy Hendrix. She died in 2007 after being addicted to slimming tablets for over thirty years. The amazingly talented Linda Jones 'You Hit Me Like TNT,' died of a diabetic attack, after collapsing just off stage, during a performance at the Apollo theatre. The Contours were not the luckiest of groups, Hubert Johnson committed suicide in July 1981 by swallowing rat poison and lead vocalist Billy Johnson ended up in prison through drug related charges. Florence Ballard of the Supremes died of a heart attack aged just 32. The Temptations must rate as one of the most tragic groups with regards to mortality. Apart from Otis Williams the rest of the members have died quite prematurely. Eddie Kendrick died of lung cancer aged 52. Paul Williams shot himself in a parked car. Melvin Franklin died of a brain seizure also aged 52. David Ruffin died in a shroud of mystery connected with a possible drugs overdose, he was only 50. Mary Wells died of cancer of the larynx aged 49. Gladys Knight almost cut off her tongue when she fell from a table while licking icing sugar off a sharp kitchen knife. She also blew $45000 at a Vegas Casino one night. Berry Gordy intended to release 'Tomorrow and Always,' by the Satintones, as his first record for his new label 'Motown.' This had to be withdrawn from distribution when Gordy was threatened with a hefty lawsuit which claimed copyright infringement of The Shirelles original hit. Bill Withers used to fit toilets on Jumbo jets.

CHAPTER 19

You've Been Leading Me On

When you're a beginner on the Northern Soul scene, it was very easy to become confused when it came to buying records. I decided to build a record collection so I didn't have to wait until Saturday to hear my own music. The record dealers who gathered around the downstairs bar of the Casino gave an air of superiority. Not purposely by any means, more the fact that I respected that they had each built these phenomenal collections. Apart from the cost involved there was the knowledge that coincided with the ownership. It took time to learn who the artists were or what the title of a record was. Cover ups were the DJ's way of keeping a records identity hidden and to be honest this mattered little to me. Those cover ups were going to be something that when revealed, would cost a high amount of cash. My record collection would be starting with the basics, mostly pressings and the easy to get hold of originals. Motown Classics that crossed in to Northern Soul were plentiful and gave your record collection some prestige. As I became an avid collector I started to pick out certain tunes that I would spend hours searching through boxes for. Sometimes I hardly knew the full title I was searching for and on other occasions, I would only know the artist. One night at the Casino I heard 'The Close She Gets,' by John Drevars Expression. It had been getting played over the past few weeks and on the bus home we asked if anyone had picked up who it was and what it was called. Someone on the bus sang out loud, 'who's that girl over there, the one with the sun in her hair.' That was it, no one had any idea of who sang it or the real title. Later that week I visited Wigan market and was browsing through records on a market stall. This stall catered for all tastes but I had found a few northern soul records on the odd occasion. My record collection at home had now grown to be what I would call, above average. I'd paid some handsome money for certain records and I was now looking to find more obscure sounds. I had convinced myself that there were rare hidden gems amongst these crates of scratched vinyl, that these ordinary record sellers didn't know they possessed. While on a trip to Notting Hill in London, I'd come across a record shop based in an old Victorian house where you literally walked on records such was the volume that was held in the property. I had managed to dig out some great finds, such as, 'Turn the Beat Around,' Vicki, Sue Robinson, on 12 inch. 'Brainstorm, 'Loving is Really My Game,' twelve inch, with a strange message scratched in to the vinyl on the clear centre run off. It said something like 'if this is a hit it will be a miracle.' But rather than looking as if scratched in by hand, it looked more deliberate, as if done at the stage of production. I picked up a bag full of Northern, and clearly remember not being charged anything extravagant. As I searched hopefully through the market trader's records, I scanned for anything that was in a white cardboard sleeve. This would be a giveaway with regards to the record possibly belonging once to a collector. The title would be written clearly in black marker at the top left-hand corner. Then in a paper sleeve I came across what I thought was nothing short of a miracle. Just like I predicted the hapless trader let me have my find for the going rate of any ordinary record. Lightly scuffed with a couple of scratches I now had in my hands on an orange label 'The Girl with the Sun in Her Hair.' I raced home, well actually, I bussed it home, very slowly, but excited to throw this lucky find straight on to my record player. When I finally got the needle down and this 45 spinning, it suddenly hit me between the ears and between the legs. I had inadvertently purchased the music used in the Sun-silk hair spray advert. The girl with the sun in her hair was the one who had enough lacquer to fight off a hurricane. Years later I sold my collection and it's not so much the fact that I no longer have the records that I loved, it's more the history of how I obtained them that I miss. Each record represented an accomplishment, a search with a quest fulfilled. Taking a record out of its sleeve would trigger a memory along with the label and the song itself. Like the famous time machine in the 1960 film starring Rod Taylor, the spinning disc could propel you to a specific moment back in time. My parting shot on this subject would be to say, for all the great records that I had and sold, there was a great big pile of shit to match. I had this theory that if people liked Joe 90, they may like the sound of some failed old record or B side that no one had considered. Isn't that how the Lords of the turntables did it? Wasn't this a page out of Ian Levine's book? No, it was actually a page out of a fairy tale that started, 'once upon a time,' and ended up with, 'and the dickhead threw it in the bin.' The only Gamble in the Casino that paid off was Lenny Gamble aka Tony Blackburn, 'I'll do Anything,' on Casino Classics. Yes, that's 'classics,' so who could blame me for trying. I wonder if I could get Zoe Ball to cover 'Cheating Kind,' by Don Gardner and give her a pseudonym such as Doris Holloway, or Fat Ball Slim. I remember one Christmas the DJ's had got together and created a list of the top ten records played that year. They played each one in succession with a jovial festive spirit. Yet it felt like a scant disregard to their faithful. The flavour came across to me as if they were saying, 'we can't believe you let us play this.' I remember 'Black Power,' James Coit, being the number one turkey, with Muriel Day's, 'Nine Times Out of Ten,' somewhere in the count down. At the time, they were floor packers and even as they were being announced and played as fodder, the floor still packed out to each one. Too late, we had been brain washed and conditioned to react faithfully to the music. 'The Manchurian candidate,' springs to mind, or for the younger reader, think of the church scene in 'The Kingsmen.' I purchased 'Nine Times

Out of Ten,' on a reddish perhaps aptly named label called 'Skunk,' At the time I felt like the proud owner of a real floor filler. Talking of a creature that leaves you with a bad smell, which DJ first played Tony Blackburn's, 'I'll Do Anything?' 'Will the real Slim Shady please stand up, please stand up.' Another one of Tony Blackburn's records that managed to get a few spins was called, 'It's Only Love Trying to Get Through.' On the MGM label, I purchased this knowing it was Tony Blackburn and I thought it was better than his alter ego Lenny Gamble. Trying to recall the other records that attributed to this Christmas list of shame is quite difficult, but I believe that 'The Joker Went Wild,' Brian Hyland, and 'Stop Girl,' Seven Dwarfs, were the only others I genuinely remember. Here's the sixty-four-dollar question, If Tony Blackburn was good enough to be on the 'Casino Classics,' label, why was he not asked to sing at the Casino? This brings us nicely on to 'Blue Eyed Soul.'

◆ ◆ ◆

CHAPTER 20

Blue Eyed Soul

Of the many records played at the Casino one could be forgiven for thinking, this just doesn't sound like Soul. Not only is it missing that unmistakable ethnicity, it also lacks the raw vocal power that defines it its very nature. On occasion some may even ask, 'isn't that the same white guy who sings 'Big Girls Don't Cry?' Many of us would associate soul music bursting from the lungs of black people who have a legacy to its ownership. 'Pretty Little Thing Let Me Light Ya Candle Cos Mama I'm Sure Hard to Handle Now yes Sir Am.' Over to Lenny Gamble to get that cover version sorted. How about, 'My People Work in Chains,' Black Power, James Coit. Maybe one for Len Barry, slight twist on the lyrics obviously. How about, 'My People Work in Chain Stores?' The thing that makes Northern Soul work, is its blatant disregard for part of its title. The word 'Northern' has given this music the licence to twist the rules beyond the requirements of any hallmarks. Peggy March sits in the same box as Lavern Baker, as does R Dean Taylor next to Frank Wilson. This music can go from a scintillating heartfelt Eddie Spencer, asking, 'If This Is Love,' to The Rainbow People, 'Living in A Dream World, with almost a theatrical feel. Both of these can sit happily side by side on the same decks of any Northern Soul DJ. Instrumentals are also synonymous with the play lists of Northern Soul, highly orchestral and flamboyant with lots of strings and brass. Kiki Dee, Helen Shapiro and Dusty Springfield are still floating people across the dance floors of all-nighters every weekend and have stood the test of time. The phrase often used by DJ's at the Casino when introducing certain records would be 'Blue Eyed Soul.' Not so much an apology just a way of saying 'maybe not what you expected.' Cliff Bennet and the Rebel Rousers, belting out 'Got to a Get You into My Life.' works, but for a reason, far beyond justification. Just for the record, here's a few other well-known artists that would make the typical 'Blue Eyed Soul,' play list. *Paul Anka, Spencer Davis, Bobby Goldsboro, Gary Lewis, Wayne Gibson, Jackie Trent, Shane Martin* and there are many more. All the above could be added to a CD and marketed as Northern Soul Classics and there could be no argument. Soul music without a single black artist? Lloyd Bradley the author of 'Soul On CD,' gave an in-depth interpretation to the meaning of Soul during the introduction of his book. He writes, 'it's a black thing, why? Because the development of that music cannot be separated from the social/economic changes within black America.' This comprehensive book bares no mention of Gary Lewis and the Playboys or Bobby Goldsboro and, why would it?

CHAPTER 21

The Collectors

The bigger your box the bigger the attraction, especially if it was made of teak. Within the contents of those boxes were the sounds of young America, and the lost dreams of the long forgotten. In 1955 seven of America's top fifteen best-selling pop records had their roots in rhythm and blues. Records produced primarily for a black audience struck a chord with white teenagers. They rushed out and purchased the duplicated version made by white artists, instead of the original recordings by black artists. This was due to the air play that white artists received on the many US racially segregated radio stations. This meant The Maguire Sisters were at number one with 'Sincerely,' while the original recording by the Moonglows, was nowhere to be seen. This unfortunately happened to many black artists of the time, they understandably felt they were suffering from an unfair competition, as did their record companies. Those producers were mostly small independent operations without the power and influence of the major labels. Atlantic, the top selling R & B label at the time, were particularly unhappy about the proliferation of white copies, or cover versions as they were known. They would complain that radio stations were falling over themselves to play Georgia Gibbs version of 'Tweedle Dee,' while listeners were not given the chance to hear the original version by Laverne Baker. Consequently, giving Gibbs a hit record due to this unfair system. Years later Northern Soul DJ's brought to life these long forgotten artists and obscure labels through their single-minded intuition. All based on a gut feeling that they had found a record that had all the qualities needed for the Northern scene. One can only imagine the pride they experienced as they broke a rare old gem, to an audience which demanded a certain quality. I remember those DJ's introducing and breaking a new record, with a few hopeful words and a possibly crossed fingers. One record I remember being played for the first time at the Casino was 'Happy,' Velvet Hammer. A quiet introduction building slowly with a very soft vocal, it was met with an empty dance floor. If tumble weed had of rolled across that floor it would not have been out of place. The faithful would look bemused and contemplate on its worthiness. A juke box jury that voted with their feet. It would take a couple of plays for a decision to be made, but the Velvet Hammer eventually hit the nail on the head and the crowd were united in their approval. It needed some perseverance and I would guess some self-belief to break a record, as an empty dance floor could take some time to resurrect. But without that gritty determination, would we have had the pleasure of hearing and owning so many iconic tunes? I could never understand why people could visit an art gallery and stand in front of a painting and discuss its content with such passion. A Picasso to me was a misshaped face, very much in the likeness of Pepper Pig. Van Goch painted like a four-year-old and 'The Scream,' by Edward Munch, looks like an alien who's running away from a Grace Jones concert. Show me a record label and I could stare at it for ages. Show me a record label with the words, 'demo,' or 'not for sale, radio station copy, 'and I'd be intrigued. Printed on that label was the DNA, and history of its origin. The record label itself is basically a trademark, its putting information regarding the owner and copyright all over it. The buyer sees the brand name, the title and the name of the group or singer. Surrounding that information, is a whole heap of other product facts that are more important to the record company than the buyer. Most standard 45 rpm records between the 1950's and

60's era gave the same basic details, which would include, length in time for record to play. The producer, the publisher, the writer of the music in small print if not the actual singer or performer. The registered trademark information and were the record was pressed. Sometimes this would be the state or just the country and very often the date the record was manufactured. For the real avid collectors, there are matrix codes stamped into the dead wax which to most people mean nothing. These series of numbers you can see in the run off part of the vinyl towards the centre of the record and are produced by a metal stamp to indicate to the studio how many they've published. Some collectors who have serious ambitions of getting hold of exact first editions, will use this stamp for verification. From my scant knowledge and for reasons that hold little interest to me, I believe it may have something to do with tax. I promised at the start of this book that I wouldn't fall in to geek territory and I already have. My purpose from the outset was to unravel a few myths and to explain how I never fully understood the culture I belonged to. With that in my mind and wanting to get back on the right track, I only recently discovered why most of the records I had bought had a great big hole in the centre. Again, I never questioned this I happily clipped in to that record a plastic centre. This large hole in the centre of the record was incorporated so that they could be played easily on jukeboxes. I was staggered when I read this as it was something that I'd never questioned. For those people who are fortunate to still own a healthy collection of Northern Soul records, then it would probably contain the likes of some very well-known labels. Standard bearers such as, Ric Tic, Okeh, Stateside, Vee Jay, Kent and Swan, to name but a few. The brits had become accustomed to buying their music on labels such as, EMI, Bell and Polydor, who were the main distributors of a large proportion of the top charting vinyl. Northern Soul labels were mainly obscure and often a bland affair when it came to art work, a good collection would boast a variety of unusual names and designs. But there were also labels that had the more prominent American artists signed to them and it was possible to hear four or five great songs attached to one familiar label. Cameo Parkway was a major contributor that helped provide a rich source of classic Northern sounds. Created by two song writers from Philadelphia, Bernard Lowe and Kal Mann, their first success came with 'Butterfly,' by Charlie Gracie. They managed to sign up the teenage sensation Bobby Rydell, who at the age of seventeen gave Cameo Parkway a high profile. Another big signing included Chubby Checker who went on to become world renown. 'The Twist,' hitting number one across the globe and creating a dance craze to enforce its sales. It should also be said that Checker was an amazing singer in his own right, with 'You Just Don't Know,' being adopted by the Soul scene across the U.K. We also have Cameo Parkway to thank for recording artists such as, Vicky Baines, Bobby Paris, Dee Dee Sharpe and Yvonne Baker, who's 'You Didn't Say a Word,' manages to raise the hairs on the neck every time. Synonymous with everything Northern Soul and finding its way on to bags, badges and even tattoos, is the celebrated 'Okeh,' label. A classic label that originated as early as 1918 and founded by Otto K. E. Heineman, using his initials to create a famous home to many talented black artists. Many prominent musicians have lent their talents to this outstanding New York based label and they include, Walter Jackson, Larry Williams, Major Lance and The Artistic's. During the fifties, the talents of Count Basie and Duke Ellington kept the label at the forefront of the music industry having the two legendary jazz men on its books at the same time. 'Okeh,' is a label that has boomed and bust over the decades with regards to its financial standing. In an ever-competitive market, it was important to create and discover talent in order to remain somewhere near the surface of the saturated record business. During the early part of the sixties, Okeh wasn't living up to its name and the label was struggling along with many others during a quiet recession. The arrival of Carl Davies as a producer was to signal better times ahead, and when Curtis Mayfield joined in 1962 as co-producer the label began to prosper quickly. The combined writing of both these men provided hits for many artists which continued until they both departed in 1966. Once again, this famous label found itself struggling and eventually closed its doors in 1970. Since then it has been re-launched by Sony in 1994 only to close again in 2000. Remarkably it started up again as a jazz label in 2013. It would seem that 'Okeh,' refuses to be 'KO'd.' We now come to a label that has so much history that a volume of books would be needed to recount its enormity. Looking back at my notes from 1998, I can see that I had realised that to incorporate the almighty 'Motown,' label into my writing was not going to be an easy task to undertake. I wanted to encapsulate its wealth of history in a brief but respectful account. I initially thought that this would take a vast amount of time and this was something I had little of. Three young children and a full-time job, including plenty of overtime certainly limited my resources. I read how I was contemplating throwing a sickie to get off work with the aim of spending some extra time writing. I'm sure Roald Dahl never had to even consider such actions. As a matter of fact, Roald Dahl spent his time writing in his garden shed from 10am to midnight every day until he had completed whatever book he was working on. He once wrote 'we have so much time and so little to do, no strike that reverse it.' Thoughts of placing my foot under a passing fork lift truck with the win win situation of a sizeable claim and a long spell off work had crossed my mind. It may have crossed my mind but I was not stupid enough to let something that weighs an average of 5,000 pounds cross my foot. I imagined the pain involved and dropped that idea quickly. I then got the break I needed in more ways than one. I broke my leg playing football. It was a bad break too and I was to spend some considerable time hospitalised and totally screwed. Two screws in fact through my left Tibia (ouch) which duly became infected and added more time to my recuperation. Two months of lying on my arse and connected to a drip was not the circumstances I'd imagined. The guy who'd broken my leg was actually on my team, now there's something that doesn't happen every day. If he wanted me out of the team why didn't he just say. I actually drove myself to hospital not believing I was about to be trollied into theatre. As the saying goes, 'be careful what you wish for.' I read in my journal, that after a few weeks in bed, I had been subjected to a bed bath by two young female nurses and at one point had remarked that I was singing 'take away the pain stain,' by Patti Austin. I doubt that very much and I would hazard a guess that if I was singing anything it would have been The Yum Yums, Gonna be a Big Thing.' Maybe not. So, time was now on my side and I wrote a mass of predictable Motown clichés. 'My description of 'The sound of young America,' became an A to Z of everything we already knew. I read Berry Gordy's autobiography that was given to me by a friend and writer George Orr. He was another person who told me to get this book done thirty years ago. We both worked in a hell hole of a factory, but George had written a trio of successful books charting the history of Everton football club. He was a big Bob Dylan fan too and wrote a book on the history of Dylan. Although we supported the same team, I could never understand the huge following Bob Dylan had amassed. A massive worldwide fan base and credited by so many other artists with providing musical inspiration. Apart from 'Lay Lady Lay,' I thought the rest of his repertoire sounded like 'twenty drunken greats.' But isn't that what sets us apart? There is the Bob Dylan, that I know for a handful of songs and the Bob Dylan that the real fans know in-depth. The Berry Gordy autobiography told me about an entrepreneur who built an empire, how he did it and who was in it. Interesting to a point, but no more interesting than Stings autobiography or Terry Wogans, which both I have read. 'Motown' to some is Diana Ross, 'Baby Love,' Diana Ross to Northern Soul, is 'Stormy,' and 'Nathan Jones.' Stevie Wonder was and still is a massive 'Motown,' legend. Yet, to Northern Soul, he is 'Uptight,' and 'Nothings too Good for My Baby.' The one fundamental condition in the world of Northern Soul is, not all 'Motown,' fits the bill. The biggest names don't necessarily provide the biggest hits. 'Can I Get A witness,' 'Ain't That Peculiar,' and 'This Loved Starved Heart of Mine,' and a couple of other minor records, is as far as it goes with Marvin Gaye's contribution. However, when asked what his own personal favourite record was that he'd recorded, I was surprised to hear it was 'Little Darling.' Both this and the Flirtations version were equally as popular on the scene and to be fair equally as good. Trying desperately to steer clear of writing long lists of titles and artists I have to concede that I have no choice but to mention the big hitters that will remain the 'Motown,' anthems now and forever at an all-nighter. 'When I'm Gone,' Brenda Holloway, 'You're Gonna Love My Baby,' Barbara McNair, 'Just A Little Misunderstanding,' The Contours, and of course 'Do I Love You,' Frank Wilson. The late great Edwin Starr has possibly more records played at all-nighters under the 'Motown,' umbrella than any other artist. The degrees of separation are marginal, but it's because of those fine margins that you won't hear, 'I Want You Back,' The Jackson Five. Thanks to the vision of Berry Gordy and a loan of $800 dollars back in 1959, we can enjoy an incredible variation of lesser known 'Motown,' music. Originally launched as 'Tamla,' it had its first release with Marv Johnson's, 'Come to Me.' Later Gordy changed the label to 'Tamla Motown,' derived from 'Motor Town, Detroit. By 1965 the independently run label was the biggest selling record company in the United States. Outselling Capitol records who had the Beatles selling all over America at this time. Gordy expanded his ever-increasing empire by bringing out other labels and buying out any others that posed as a threat to his business. Subsidiary labels created through 'Motown,' were, 'Soul, VIP, Ric Tic, Gordy and Golden World.' Together they produced an ambulance of future collectibles for the Northern Soul fan. From those humble beginnings at 2648 Grand Boulevard, were a sign proclaimed this to be the home of 'Hitsville USA,' came hit after hit. Recording at 'Motown,' during the sixties were artists and groups that maybe were not as much of a household name as their contemporaries. Virgil Henry, Frances Nero, Linda Griner along with The Originals, The Monitors and The Andantes, were not as commonly known in the U.K. These artists became rich pickings for the Northern Soul scene and their slightly off the mark recordings didn't always catch on with the UK wider audience. Their loss was our gain and let's face it, love it or hate it, without this legendary label for which we owe so much, there would be no 'Do I Love You.' Another label that deserves a mention but takes us away from the scene but only by a few degrees is the remarkable 'Stax,' label. In some ways, one could say this famous brand of music was 'Motown's,' greatest opponent during the sixties. It's founder James F Stewart, was a bank clerk from Memphis, who played the fiddle with a few local bands. Fiddle and bank clerk don't seem to be a good choice of words in the same sentence, but Stewart was about to be involved in a set-up of his own. With an accomplice who happened to be his friend and barber, who also owned some basic recording equipment, he managed to set up a studio in his uncle's garage. His first label was called Satellite but this was short lived due to its instant success. Frank Stewart decided to expand his company and managed to persuade his sister Estelle Axton to acquire a second mortgage in order to purchase better quality equipment. Along with his sister he set up a new studio in Brunswick Memphis. This studio had the unfortunate location of being adjacent to a railway track and many recordings were ruined by the rumble of a train or the blast of a whistle. There was little success for the Brunswick studio apart from when they recorded the Veltones, 'Fool in Love.' Mercury picked up the recording for release after paying $500, but the record consequently dived and ended their relationships thereafter. In 1960 Stewart purchased the Capitol theatre in Memphis and it was from here that the business began to take off. From this studio Stewart recorded Rufus and Carla Thomas Cause I Love You,' which became a big hit. Due to this success and other hits from the father and daughter duo, Atlantic records became interested in what was taking place in Memphis. Atlantic secured a deal with Satellite and began to distribute some of its material. This was mainly Rufus and Carla's recordings, but they were released on the subsidiary Atco label rather than the Atlantic label. Some Northern Soul fans and collectors may not be aware that they probably possess many records connected to the 'Stax,' and 'Atlantic,' labels. 'I'm Coming to Your Rescue,' The Triumphs, was a big play at the Casino and this was recorded on the 'Volt,' label. This group had taken their name from a red TR-3 Triumph car, that was owned by guitarist Chips Moman, who was involved with the creation of Stax. Another famous Stax artist was the iconic Isaac Hayes who once belonged to the doo wop group the Ambassadors. The full scale of the talent that passed through the doors of the Stax studio is immeasurable. Many of the singers who came as part of a group went on to be solo artists with even more acclaim. Dave Prater of 'Sam and Dave,' started with a group called The 'Hummingbirds.' Leon Haywood, 'L.O.V.E,' was an organ player for the STAX house band 'The MG's.' As Satellite records grew in stature another company from California informed Frank Stewart that they had the sole rights to the brand name. Stewart was offered to buy the name but declined and decided to change the name to STAX, by adopting the first two letters of his surname and the first two letters of his sister's maiden name. **St**ewart & **Ax**ton. New York was the home of SUE records which was established in 1957 by Henry Juggy Murray Jones. Situated very close to the famous Apollo theatre which inevitably became a source for discovering up and coming local talent. Bobby Hendricks became the first artist to achieve some success with Sue Records with 'Itchy Twitchy Feeling,' which became a top 30 US hit. The backing vocals were supplied by the Coasters who went on to record many top US hits themselves. 'Yakety Yak,' was their biggest and most well-known hit, however on the Northern scene we took hold of 'Crazy Baby.' The volatile Ike and Tina Turner also signed for Sue records proving to be an astute and major source of income for Henry Jones's company. Don Covay was another excellent addition to the stable and also appreciated for his 'It's Better to Have.' A strange story developed with this label as it allowed some of its recordings to be sold in the U.K. on the

Decca owned London label. London records fell into the hands of a DJ by the name of Guy Stevens who was given license to release artists through other labels. The plot thickens. It was decided that Stevens was releasing sub-standard music on subsidiary labels and the control was given back to Jones. By the late sixties Sue records began to lose its piece of the market and when a proposed deal with STAX failed, Jones was left with no alternative but to sell. He sold all the masters to United Artists, but managed to keep the rights to the name Sue. He decided to form a new label and gave it the name of 'Jupiter. Keeping with the 'big Apple,' Buddha records was a company formed by Neil Bogart, formerly of Cameo Parkway. This unique label grossed five million dollars in its first year of trading. It became the owner of the Karma Sutra catalogue which distributed Curtis Mayfield's Windy C and Curtom labels. A major signing for Buddha was Gladys Knight and the Pips, from Motown. The labels mentioned previously would only be the tip of the iceberg if it came down to compiling an in-depth list of the labels found in a serious collector's record box. There are literally thousands of labels to choose from and they would include the well-known Mirwood, Thelma, Chess, to the less well known such as El Camino or Colony. Behind each label there will be a fascinating story of its humble beginnings and its ownership. From hundreds of towns and cities across America there sprung countless small enterprises with a label that would disaster as quickly as they started. They provided Northern Soul with a catalogue of obscurities that came about in some cases by design and in others by default.

◆ ◆ ◆

CHAPTER 22

It's All Over

1981 heralded what was to be the final chapter of the Casino's history. As Bob Dylan had famously written, 'The Times They are a Changing.' They were indeed changing; Wigan Council were about to start the ball rolling on some major construction projects. But, before any of these development plans could be auctioned, certain places needed to be earmarked for demolition. One of those buildings selected for destruction happened to be the Casino. With the promise of better things to come, the council had a golden opportunity to get rid of what they believed was a wart on the face of Wigan. At the same time, it has to be said that the Casino was struggling to pull in even a quarter of the numbers it once had in its earlier years. It had started to lose its vitality and the wall of sound was now reverberating around this old decaying building. Selfishly I enjoyed the nights of low attendance with the room to move freely and the push and shove now like no forgotten. The Empress as she was formerly known was beginning to feel her age with creaking joints and a crumbling exterior. The oldies all-nighters that took place once a month on a Friday, were pulling in the biggest crowds. The Saturday that followed the oldies were painfully low in attendance. The once faithful crowd had found that the other avenues of life had begun to pull them in to different directions. Relationships, unemployment, travel and in some cases marriage and children. New members were short in supply and as numbers dwindled so did the coaches and the larger traveling groups. These were the people that were likely to encourage new blood to the all-nighter. The introduction of a more modern crossover sound to the dance floor did not appeal to everyone. I remember hearing comments were certain records were greeted with despair. 'This is Disco,' became a familiar comment. I heard this from the more mature members. Who could blame them, especially if their roots where in 'The Wheel,' or 'The Torch.' 'It Takes Heart, So Many Sides of You, Lovin is Really My Game, Janice, Lady in Red, all these tunes were taking the Casino in a different direction. The dancing styles were changing and the fashion statements was more modern. I personally liked the mix of the old with the new and those modern sounds are now considered as classics today. 'Love is a Serious Business,' Alfie Davidson, is a game changer when it comes to filling an empty dance floor in today's venues. I remember being at the Casino when it was first played, I told my friend I thought it was Elton John. There were other outside influences to consider with the loss of numbers to the Casino and one of those was the Iron Lady. Margaret Thatcher had turned the North and south divide into something that had a detrimental effect on anyone living north of Watford. The Toxteth riots had almost brought Mrs Thatcher to write off Liverpool and it is thought that she was prepared to let the city sink in its own waste. She had thought about arming the police but stopped short of issuing that order. To quell the disturbance, she gave permission for the police to fire rubber bullets at rioters for the first time on British soil. The political divides grew daily as the harsh realities of the poorer northern locations became increasingly apparent. Starved by cutting down on industry, yet encouraged to buy their houses the ticking time bomb of debt, exploded in the face of the working man in the severest manner. Bailiffs were working around the clock repossessing houses as the boom and bust businesses fell apart. It was estimated that 100,000 houses per week were being taken away from their owners. The yuppie had been born and quaffed champagne without a care for anything other than increasing their portfolios and carrying a Filofax. They later felt the wrath of indignation when it became regular news that yet another entrepreneur had decided to jump off a building in Paternoster Square, the home of the London Stock Exchange. They too had invested greedily in the Tory waltzer, a ride full of spin with a disoriented ending. While three quarters of the country sat in front of the TV and sympathised with Alan Bleasdale's 'Boys from the Black stuff', the others took advantage of those that had become unemployed. Cheap labour was standing at the edge of every kerb hoping for a day's work with cash in hand. If, like four million other people you happened to be on the dole, then Norman Tebbit's advice was to get on your bike and look for work. Just for the record, if anyone happens to actually be acquainted with Mr Tebbit, please let him know we couldn't even afford a bike. In reference to a House of Lords debate 4th July 2014, the honourable Mr Tebbit has now started to condemn cyclists for their behaviours and wearing headphones. I guess most of them are on their way to work Mr Tebbit and not polluting the rest of London. Unlike like some who complained recently about how long it takes to get from Parliament Square to the Tower of London in a car. I suggest you take your own advice and 'Get on your bike,' Lord Tebbit.' In 1981 luxury money became scarce and a giro was the only source of income for many people. This probably had an adverse effect on the numbers attending the Casino. Being able to travel long distance and afford entrance fees was based on the youth of the day having a job and extra cash flow. For me the dole queue was a reality which meant a fortnightly trip of shame and embarrassment. It was a queue that stretched endlessly around the main council building known as Whelmar House. The queues that were divided alphabetically by surname continued outside the building and around a corner and straight past the job centre. You would be asked if you had worked since you last signed on and the same answer passed from every person's lips. The job centre had less cards displaying possible employment than the cards in shops selling belongings. For the unskilled there was nothing to choose from. The majority of cards were looking for highly qualified individuals with qualifications in trades. My empty pockets had drained the Casino from my list of priorities and the offers to work away from home became impossible to refuse. Working on building sites all over the country usually included Saturday and Sunday's and therefore weekends were spent drinking and sleeping rough on site. Rumours of the Casinos closure had started to gain momentum; however, this was something that we had grown accustomed to over the years. When the decision to end the Casino was finalised and a date for closure became a reality it was met with quiet acceptance. Inevitably the announcement went out advertising what was going to be the last night of the Casino. I had a belief that another announcement would soon follow, saying 'Casino rescued from closure,' but I had lost touch with the real inside story. The threats of closure had fallen into the myth category and it wasn't until I heard that tickets had gone on sale that I accepted the myth had become a reality. On Saturday, September the 19th 1981, the last all-nighter was to take place and it would be an occasion that would be etched on the memory of anyone who attended. To say, 'I was there,' would be a phrase owned by only a select few. Or would it?

I can't remember where I was the night of the 19th but I would hazard a guess that I was proving up some labour club bar, head spinning and about to shovel down a kebab on the way home. I can't believe that I didn't think to buy a ticket, I wasn't there, but I wish I was. But the ugly truth was, that this wasn't to be the last all-nighter and many of the Casino faithful were to be slapped in the face with another end of an era night. The reason behind this audacious new last all-nighter we were told, was to accommodate those unfortunate people who couldn't attend the last all-nighter or were locked out on the night. Or maybe, happened to be working on the 19th, or had been propping up the bar at a labour club. So, it was decided to have the really, definitely, swear to god, no fingers crossed behind the back, last all-nighter. Now everybody can retire happy on the 2nd of October, that is apart from those who went on the 19th of September. If you are one of those who went on the 19th can I just say, it's a bit like you went to the dress rehearsal. Did I just rub salt in that wound, my apologies? Did this make a mockery of those who genuinely thought they would make that one last trip? Or, was this a sincere attempt to please those fans who really wanted to attend the last all-nighter but couldn't get a ticket? A very sad state of affairs and one that makes me glad that I was breaking my back carrying bricks on a building site. Sweating ten hours a day for a pitiful wage. Sarcasm? Some of the people who travelled to Wigan on the 19th would have travelled many miles just to have had the privilege to be a part of something that had touched their lives. Worse was yet to come, like a wounded bull the Casino was trotted out again on the 6th of December. People had suffered from enough 'bull,' and it was now exhausted, tired and in need of the tercio de muerte (third of death). This is where the matador kills the bull by putting a sword between is shoulders and straight into its heart. The heart of soul fell on its knees that night and its attendance was nothing like the two-previous end of an era all-nighters. Not surprisingly the Casino breathed its last on the 6th of December, and its final fate was about to throw up even more controversy. Was the management trying desperately to keep the all-nighters alive or was this a money based decision? Where they like a condemned man hoping for a last-minute reprieve or was it a selfish act of poor judgement. It became a sore point for many fans. Sadly, there were no winners, just losers and it became apparent that the Casino had held its genuine last all-nighter. I often wonder, if the Casino could have made some links with local charities, thus helping it to be seen in a better light. There may have been charitable collections and worthy donations at the time, but I don't recall seeing or hearing of any. In my home town in North Wales, many Northern Soul nights are in aid of local charities. Perhaps more compassion towards the Casino from the local authorities would have been gained had they have adopted the same principle. In return, this could have helped lessen the burden and stigma attached from the negative press relating to drugs. It sounds somewhat like a selfish ploy to gain favour, it worked for Pablo Escobar. Okay, not the best analogy, but I'm sure you get the drift. Today, were the Casino once stood, is the Grand Arcade shopping centre built in 2007. No rushing the council on the start date. Before its construction, there stood a big empty space that was, well, 'a waste of space.' The café in the Grand Arcade is themed in honour of the Casino, with a plaque on a wall with the words, 'On this site stood, the world famous northern soul club.' It should also say, flattened 31 years ago, in preparation for today's cup of tea. Wigan lost a part of its heritage and had it of been rescued, would have made a great exhibition site. Today's entrepreneurial thinking people would have bid the roof off the Casino, had it have been put up for auction. Think, Hard Rock Café, or Graceland and the Elvis fans who travel the world to stand in the home of their idol. Wigan Pier was the subject of much investment twenty years ago, hoping to bring in visitors based on nothing more than a George Orwell novel and a satirical misconception. It has now closed down. I've been to the Wigan Pier and it's not the most exciting place in the north tha knows. It once had a Victorian class room experience and it can only be compared to eating black pudding. You know what it is, you still eat it, but part of you wishes you hadn't.

◆ ◆ ◆

Headline News

Wigan Observer; Thursday 6th August 1981

End of the road for the Casino All-nighter. Wigan's famous Casino All-Nighters and Oldies nights are to end for good next month.

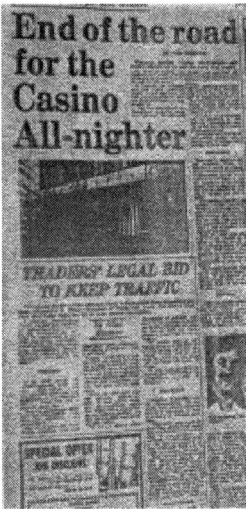

DJ Russ Winstanley, who founded the celebrated All-Nighters back in 1973 gave the shock announcement this week which will be a severe blow to thousands of northern Soul fans throughout the country. He blamed the recession and club's uncertain future for the shutdown, to take place immediately after the final All-Nighter on September 10. 'The club has suffered tremendously from the recession,' he said, 'we used to get people traveling from places like Scotland every fortnight, but now it costs £30 to £40 to get to Wigan from there now and with there being so little money around they started coming only every two months or so. 'It's hit a lot of Wiganers too. On Saturday, we once had over 1,000 regularly turning up, but recently it's dropped to around 600. Although Friday nights are still packed, there's been a combination of factors brought it to an end. **IMPOSSIBLE Russ** said he could not see the recession lifting and thought it would be impossible to carry on in the present circumstances. He also voiced concern for the legion of fans and supporters of the Casino Oldies and All-Nighters who will now be deprived of what was for so long their musical home. 'It's like being kicked in the stomach,' he said. We all feel the same. It's the end of an era and there'll be a lot of tears shed when we tell everybody the sad news this weekend. For eight years it's been very much a part of people's lives and now it's over.' Russ felt bitter that what had virtually become an institution, thanks mainly to the unceasing efforts of both he and club owner Gerry Marshal, had now been forced to shut its doors through circumstances beyond his control. The Casino had put Wigan on the map when it began its series of All-Nighter soul discos almost eight years to the shutdown, on September 23, 1973. **FOCUSED** It quickly focused attention on the phenomenon of Northern Soul which although rarely appearing in the charts had a vast underground following of young fans who would faithfully travel from all over the country just to converge in Wigan for eight hours on a Saturday night and dance continuously to otherwise obscure records. Throughout the 70's Wigan Casino became synonymous with baggy trousers, Northern Soul and the Chosen Few who had a top ten with 'Footsee,' stunning the nation watching top of the pops with their spins, back flips and leaps. The Punk music revolution in 1977 took its toll however and the Casino began to look like a pale imitation of its old self to the outside world. But the 'faithful' carried on and numerous threats to the buildings existence until this week's announcement. Russ added though that the Casino would run as normal up to September shut down and hoped that the Casino spirit would still continue and perhaps emerge in a different form in the future. 'There'll always be a Northern Soul scene,' he said 'and hopefully we might be trying some sort of Casino road show. We'll always be looking to keep the Northern scene going because it's such a great scene. It's tragic about the Casino closure after eight great years, but it seems that all good things come to an end.

Author; Regarding the statement that the Punk rock era took its toll, I very much doubt this carried any weight. Such was the great division in the type of music that separates Northern Soul from Punk. I seriously believe that no one would swap or leave the scene if they truly were a Northern Soul fan. You can't go from Frankie Beverly and the Butlers to the Sex Pistols overnight. One thing Russ did get right, which was a bold statement

at the time, was, 'there will always be a Northern Soul scene.'
How right you were Mr Winstanley.

Headline News

Wigan Observer; September 15, 1978

Wigan Casino to be demolished

Wigan's heart of soul – the Casino Club – will be demolished in two year's time.

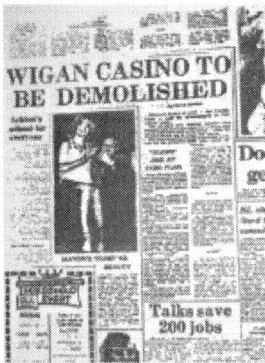

The all-night Soul dancing sessions that

brought both fame and notoriety to Wigan will end September 1980 at the latest – when the Council intend not to renew the license. The area round the Casino is included in the site for the proposed £12M civic centre extension. People from all over the country have made a regular weekly 'pilgrimage' to the All-Nighter which is due to celebrate its fifth anniversary on September 23. Despite its popularity with Britain's Soul fans the All-Nighter also brought notoriety to the town amid the rumours of drug-taking and court cases involving Soul fans and possession of drugs. **CLEAR Wigan** Casino boss Gerry Marshal recently made an offer for the Barge Inn, which closed recently, but he was unsuccessful.

Mr Marshall was away on business yesterday, but a council spokesman said: 'The Casino is included in the area shown in the planning application to indicate that the ultimate is to have an area of clear buildings entirely surrounding the completed new building.' **LICENCE** 'The actual building to be considered does not physically encroach on the Casino and construction of the civic centre can commence without interfering with the current use of the Casino. The license of the Casino expires in September 1980 and it is not intended that it should be renewed. The building will then be demolished.'

Author; As you can see from this interview the intention to get rid of the Casino was set in motion long before the last all-nighter took place. Just to be clear, that was the last one in December, not September. The Wigan Council where not secretive about their plans and progress was their intention. They knew that this old famous historic building that provided pleasure to thousands of people week in year out needed to be replaced. They could see the future, a civic hall, a car park, or may be a shopping centre. Or maybe the equivalent of a black hole. Just like a black hole, nothing came out of it, not for thirty years at least. If only the late Professor Hawkin had visited Wigan, the answer to space, black holes and relativity was sitting right be-neath the old site of the Casino. Scientists call it 'B theory of time,' meaning time is only an illusion. Gets complicated after that and not many people understand it. There is however some people on the Wigan Council thirty years ago who knew exactly how it worked. As the closure of the Casino began to gather momentum the newspapers took a lot of interest. Rescue plans suddenly emerged and it seemed there was a tug of war devel-oping between the council and those who wanted to keep the Casino alive. Some would be investors threw a life line but their ideas and proposals sank without a trace. The councils rope was tied around the building and they were all pulling in one direc-tion. The following articles explain some of the weird and won-derful attempts to save the Casino.

◆ ◆ ◆

Headline News

Wigan Observer: 11 March 1982

Rescue bids fail to save the Casino. Two eleventh hour bids to save the Wigan Casino Building -closed at the

end of last year when the leasing company went into liquidation failed this week and now seems certain that it will be demolished by the end of the year. The recommendation for demolition came from Mondays meeting of the planning and development committee. There is little doubt that it will be confirmed by the full Wigan Council later this month. In reaching their decision, the committee turned two 'rescue attempts' by potential lessees. One was from a local business consortium who wanted to turn the building into a 'Fun City,' with a roller skating ring, roundabouts, pool tables and rotating cylinder and a disco in the present Mr M's. The other bid was from a Nottingham man who wanted to continue the weekend All-Nighters and midweek modern dancing sessions. The decision was taken in private because of the confidential nature of the financial offers. But since Monday the council have been at pains to explain, in detail their reasons for wanting the building demolished. Deputy Planning Chairman, Councillor John Hilton, said after the meeting, 'to retain the Casino building would have involved the council in a tremendous amount of money. **SOUND.** Just to make it structurally sound would have cost us nearly £250,000, apart from maintenance, and although the local business consortium was willing to put in a considerable amount of cash, they were only interested in a ten or fifteen-year lease. 'Wigan Chief Estates and Valuation Officer, Mr Martin Smith added, 'I don't think either of the interested parties realise the full extent of the work that needs to be done at the Casino. The roof is leaking and one of the retaining walls would need completely rebuilding, apart from other major interior work. But the decision means disappointment for Dave Halliell and Frank Spencer, partners in the highly successful 'Bluto's' in Market street and Tom Bibby owner of a contract cleaning firm. They had hoped to turn the Casino into a 'Fun City' and Mr Halliwell said this week, 'I am surprised by the decision. What we had in mind would have provided a great deal of enjoyment for young people between eight and eighteen.... what will happen now is that we will have another blank space in the centre of

Wigan. I thought the Council would have jumped at the chance.' The demolition decision will inevitablyse speculation that phase 3 of the Civic Centre development, scheduled for this site is about to start. But Councillors denied that this factor influenced them, or that the much-postponed phase 3 is any nearer start.

Author; You May have noticed that this article, if set in order of the sequence of events, that should have preceded the newspaper article previously. Allow me to explain and to ensure you that you have not been the victim of a Wigan time warp. There are areas in this particular journalist write up that I feel he or she was trying to expose some disparities. For instance, 'decisions by the council were made in private' and 'councillors denied that factors influenced them' and then there is 'speculation regarding phase 3.' It's all very cloak and dagger and I should leave you to make your own decisions on what the councils real aims were. But I should also remind you, no Civic Centre was ever built. I would presume that a substantial amount of money was certainly needed to get the Casino back in shape and it was probably suffering from structural defects. What about the council money that was poured into Wigan Pier years later, surely the same consideration could have been afforded to the old Empress. The Casino wasn't the only building in and around Wigan that had seen better days, but I didn't see St Joseph's church, which had been boarded up in Wigan town centre for years, getting pulled down. Lord no. Was enough done to promote the Casino as an investment? Mr Halliwell, the would-be investor whose application was turned down also understood the 'B theory of time,' he said, 'what will happen now is we will have another blank *space* in Wigan.' It's all starting to make sense now.

Headline News

Last all-nighters were firemen (March 1982)

The last all-nighters at Wigan Casino turned out to be firemen. They were the ones in there swinging when the famous club put on its final fiery show on Tuesday night. A blaze started which started there shortly after 9pm severely damaged a section of the dance floor, the offices above, and the roof. Yet the cause of it is still unknown. However, it means that the decision taken at last week's Planning Committee to demolish the historic Wigan nightspot because of its dilapidated condition will now be accelerated. Within minutes of the fire being discovered ten pumps were on the scene including crews from as far away as Bolton and Merseyside. It was over an hour before the fire was brought under control as the blaze had severely damaged the coping stones around the roof. Wigan Metro Chief Estates and Valuations Officer Mr Martin Smith, said 'it's likely now that the demolition order will be speeded up.' Traffic wanting to use Station Road will now be diverted down Watkins street on to Crompton Street and back into Standishgate.

❖ ❖ ❖

Article

We still care for Wigan – don't we?

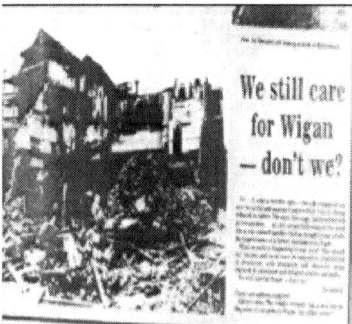

Sir- What a terrible sight- the sad remains of our once beautiful and popular Empress Hall. Now it's been reduced to rubble. The once fine stage battered beyond all recognition...An old curtain billowing in the wind like a tear stained handkerchief as though trying to hide the hopelessness of a former monument to Wigan. What on earth is happening to our town? Why should our ancient loyal town be reduced to a battlefield of desolation with desolation and character being replaced by unwanted and debatably unwanted car parks. We still care for Wigan, don't we?

From the ashes, a fire shall be woken,
A light from the shadows shall spring;
Renewed shall be blade that was broken,
The crownless again shall be king." **J.R.R. Tolkien**, **The Fellowship of the Ring**

The fire that helped to seal the fate of the Casino also helped to create its legend. The partial destruction to the building, prompted a final decision to demolish it completely. The cause of the blaze has never been identified but we must be grateful that the building was unoccupied at the time. Over its life time there was scant disregard for its occupant's safety and if any improvements were made to its structure during the Casino years, I never witnessed any. Cigarettes were flicked, thrown and left burning on the edge of tables and furnishings. Rubbish collected in large piles in the alleyways that surrounded the building. I remember the Summerland fire 1973 that happened in Douglas, Isle of Man. Fifty people lost their lives to a discarded cigarette and this was a modern building in comparison. If the fire was due to faulty wiring or some other combustible material we can only imagine the situation that may have occurred had the building been packed as it often was on an all-nighter. Thankfully that wasn't the case, but it still remains a mystery regarding the how and why it succumbed to fire. There have been the inevitable conspiracy theories regarding arson and the possibility that it was started deliberately. The initial benefactor from the fire, was the Council, having burnt the wart off the face of Wigan once and for all. But the real winner was the Casino itself and the void that ironically created a legend. If the building had gone on to be a bingo hall and still stood today, would it have held the same prominence? The reality is that there are many famous places in history that don't always have a physical presence. From the handful of pictures that exist showing the destruction of the Casino, the grand piano standing majestically on its own seems to be a poignant reminder to its glorious past. It stood alone in defiant silence. As the smoke began to clear new attempts were put together to revive the northern soul scene in Wigan and for a short time Wigan Tiffany's played host to a handful of all-nighters.

Headline News

Court blacks out new all-nighter

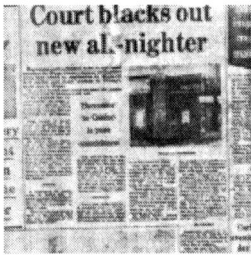

Magistrates gave a thumbs down to a planned successor for Wigan Casinos famous all-nighters when they refused an application by Mecca to hold similar Soul music sessions at Tiffany's night club in Wigan. The decision followed objections by the police who claimed that there would be problems in the town. It was highlighted that the club expected 1,000 people to attend the sessions which would start in the early hours of a Saturday morning and run until 6.30 a.m. the following day. Larger crowds of people would be gathering in the town over the week end and queuing outside the club as customers an earlier session were leaving. Mr Clifton Barker objecting to the application on behalf of the police, pointed out that drug abuse amongst teenagers had been associated with the all-night disco sessions at Wigan Casino. Crime had risen in the town and there had been clashes between local people and fans travelling in from all parts of the country. **Misuse** In addressing the magistrates Mr Barker said, 'it seems apparent that the license of Tiffany's is intending to become the successor to Wigan Casino, and my opinions are as a result of the problems this type of function at the Casino have brought.' **Successor to Casino is pure coincidence** 'You will be well aware of the drugs problem that has been introduced into the town and the number of people who regularly appeared before the courts charged with offences under the Misuse of Drugs Act. This has been introduced over the past few years while the all-night discos have been taking place at Wigan Casino. **Conflict** 'and it has caused additional problems from a criminal point of view to the police who are satisfied that many offences connected with drugs are committed by people who do in fact travel to Wigan. Cars have been taken. It was introduced a public order problem and there has been a conflict between the locals and people who travel all over the country to attend these all-night discos. Their existence has caused innumerable problems to the police which were not present before. And the fact that the club will not be licensed limits the supervision the police have on the conduct of the running of the club. Mr Milton Firman acting for Mecca, told the court that the company had already run similar events in Rotherham, Sheffield, Derby and Birmingham with great success. He said 'it is not an effort by Mecca to step in as the Casino reaches its demise. It is an attempt by the proprietor to extend his field and it is purely coincidental that the Casino is about to close. Mecca have a very credible reputation and would not wish to become a party to drug abuse or infringement of the law. Should there be any suggestion of trouble it would not be repeated. **Reviewed Magistrates** refused an application by the club for an extension of their music, singing and dancing license to cover the all-nighters. After the case, the Manager of Tiffany's Mr Russell Moore – (*end of article available*)

Author; An appeal must have taken place as I do recall visiting at least two all-nighters that took place after the Casino had closed. I also remember Tommy Hunt singing at one of those nights and getting people to dance on stage as he belted out his famous anthems. Tiffany's did a good job with top jocks, but something or someone must have thrown a spanner in the works as the new all-nighters were short lived. The town of Wigan, for so long the home of Northern Soul, finally eradicated any ties it had with the music venues that hosted all-nighters once and for all. The future of the scene looked bleak and many die-hard fans were beginning to accept that the authorities and pressure had finally took its toll. The simple truth was, that with no talisman to carry the flag, that future now lay in locations further afield. Other venues tried to pick up were the Casino had left off and places like Morecambe Pier and Warrington Parr hall gained some momentum but they too lacked sustainability. Over the years places like King George's Hall, Burnley and Keele University, made great attempts to keep the scene alive and kicking. Apart from the well-known larger venues, there were dozens of smaller clubs and pubs that pioneered new start-ups and introduced new sounds along the way. Due to the strength, depth and massive support of its followers, Northern Soul could not be confined to history. It smouldered in the ashes of the Casino for many years and eventually it reignited the flames and passion of its former glory to burn even more brightly than ever before. Today's technology has unleashed an unprecedented interest in the availability of Northern Soul and the chance to own a wealth of rare and iconic sounds. The introduction of CD's brought an exciting opportunity to amass a collection of genuine classics that would have cost a small fortune on vinyl. Now we have the ability to stream those singles and albums via many online providers. The introduction of voice controlled devices such a Google mini and Amazon Echo make the necessity to own a collection almost obsolete. How far this technology can advance is in anybody's guess, but with 3D headsets making big steps I'm waiting to be sitting in the Casino surrounded by dancers and record dealers. Don't all shout geek at once, but what I wouldn't have given for an I phone in 1978?

Ten years ago, I relocated to Llandudno, North Wales, I lived here for a short few years as a child. The North Wales coastline has a history with Northern Soul and has been long associated with its unrelenting support for the scene. They travelled religiously week in week out to Wigan Casino from places as far away as Bangor, Llandudno and Colwyn Bay. They have held this music close to their hearts through the years and today, they continue to represent the scene in large numbers. Venues are numerous including the famous Prestatyn weekenders. On any given week throughout the year it's possible to find the new and the more experienced DJ's spinning classic vinyl in well-established venues across the counties. In the seaside town of Llandudno there is a relationship with the music that has created a dedicated following. DJ''s, Ronnie Wynn, Chico, Brummie Kev, Dave Chapman, and the younger Ben Owen, are all dedicated to keeping Llandudno and the surrounding locations stepping out to the music. Charity events run monthly at the County Hotel under the banner of 'Seaside Soul,' have helped raise money for good causes including Alzheimer's and multiple sclerosis society. DJ Rob Lloyd and his wife Denise who championed the events, highlight all that is good about Northern Soul with today's generation. The same can be said of the Llandudno Rugby Club, who along with the services of Harry Pritchard have now celebrated their tenth anniversary. Harry who is no stranger to the decks has worked hard at giving new and local DJ's the opportunity to make a name for themselves. The Grand Hotel has also hosted a weekender that is growing in stature over the past few years. With guest DJ's from all over the country as well as some home grown talented DJ's, like, Calvin Lee Hughes. The scene in Llandudno and neighbouring areas is vibrant and going through a resurgence like never before. There will be many, who on reading this, who will no doubt feel the same about their own towns and cities, believing the same passion and spirit exists right on their doorstep too. The more surprising element is the growth of Northern Soul abroad. It is incredible to see holidays in Spain, Greece and even cruises dedicated to having 'Soul in the Sun.' Ex-pats talk of all-nighters in Australia and amazingly the youth of Japan have taken a keen interest. Fashion designers have created wardrobes based on the individual signature of Northern Soul clothing and accessories. Models have walked down catwalks in step to Northern Soul music performing spins and dance routines. Television adverts have picked up on the catchy riffs of certain songs and used their compulsive rhythms to promote their wares. The 'Happy Egg Company,' using 'Do I Love You, for their recent advert, and B and Q using 'Sliced Tomatoes,' Just Brothers for theirs. I almost take some exception to this, as I can't help but feel that these people are walking through consecrated ground. Ad men and women have been doing this for years and so we have to accept that Northern Soul is fair game, even using it to advertise Felix cat food. (Rubin - You've Been Away)

❖ ❖ ❖

CHAPTER 23

We Got Togetherness

I never thought I'd get old, it kind of sneaked up on me. Fortunately, there is an energy that is fuelled by a passion which can lift an ageing body almost off the floor. A skip is added to the step, like a child playing hop scotch. A dance that is lonely to behold is lost on the outside world. The music has long past the test of time and it can never be considered as something that should be discarded to history. On the contrary, today, there is a younger, intelligent group of people who are picking up the music and understanding its complexity. They are the ones who are carrying the torch and the ones who are keeping the wheels in motion. The Casino may have been reduced to dust and rubble, but the music is now hallmarked. Like gold bars in the vaults of a bank it's become a treasure that belongs to part of the nation. The case for northern Soul and its value, needs no jury. It's guilty of bringing pleasure to millions of people who fell in love with its quirky, beautiful and sometimes real soul sound. The myths and legends that have been kicked around over the years only help to endure the mystery that is Northern Soul. With the aid of the newspaper cuttings I had collected and the fact that I lived and breathed the sweaty atmosphere of the Casino, I felt there was another story to be told. I wanted to bring home the thoughts of those who were affected by the presence of the Casino. I wanted to pay homage to those people who paid the entrance fee and travelled far and wide to reach the Casino. They were the true creators of what is still an iconic moment in British music history. With a little humour, I wanted to remind us of the moments we should have stopped and taken a reality check. My heroes weren't footballers or actors or even musicians, they were DJ's who played my music for my kind. I never met or spoke to any of them, I just watched in awe as they played the rarest records in the U.K. Keep on keeping on.

'It's a sin to kill a mockingbird. Mockingbirds don't do one thing except make music for us to enjoy.'

Case closed.

Keep the faith

U

V

WIGAN CASINO

It sounded like a crack of thunder as they clapped in unison to the music. The acrid concoction of condensation and sweat fell from the ceiling like rain on to the faithful below. Northern Soul had drawn its followers from every corner of the U.K. to the historical Lancashire town of Wigan. Long before house music and rave became the by words associated with risqué and outlandish. The now famous and legendary Wigan Casino had already laid the foundation stones for later generations to emulate. Music is often defined by the culture it creates. The mysterious world of Northern Soul managed to remain hidden from the public for decades, before eventually revealing itself commercially and much against the will of its people.

Soul Club Gents

Printed in Great Britain
by Amazon